Alan Titchmarsh
how to garden

Flowers and Foliage for Cutting

Alan Titchmarsh
how to garden

Flowers and Foliage
for Cutting

BOOKS

10 9 8 7 6 5 4 3 2 1

Published in 2013 by BBC Books, an imprint of
Ebury Publishing, a Random House Group Company

The Random House Group Limited Reg. No. 954009

Addresses for companies within the Random House
Group can be found at **www.randomhouse.co.uk**

MIX

Paper from
responsible sources

FSC™ C004592

The Random House Group Limited
supports The Forest Stewardship Council
(FSC®), the leading international forest
certification organisation. Our books
carrying the FSC label are printed on
FSC® certified paper. FSC is the only
forest certification scheme endorsed by
the leading environmental organisations,
including Greenpeace. Our paper
procurement policy can be found at
www.randomhouse.co.uk/environment

A CIP catalogue record for this book is available from
the British Library.

ISBN 978 1 84 990224 3

Produced by OutHouse!
Shalbourne, Marlborough, Wiltshire SN8 3QJ

BBC BOOKS
COMMISSIONING EDITOR: Lorna Russell
PROJECT EDITOR: Nicholas Payne
PRODUCTION: Rebecca Jones

OUTHOUSE!
COMMISSIONING EDITOR: Sue Gordon
SERIES EDITOR & PROJECT EDITOR: Polly Boyd
SERIES ART DIRECTOR: Robin Whitecross
CONTRIBUTING EDITOR: Julia Cady
DESIGNERS: Heather McCarry, Louise Turpin
ILLUSTRATIONS by Julia Cady, Lizzie Harper, Susan Hillier,
Janet Tanner
PHOTOGRAPHS by Jonathan Buckley except where
credited otherwise on page 96
CONCEPT DEVELOPMENT & SERIES DESIGN:
Elizabeth Mallard-Shaw, Sharon Cluett

Colour origination by Altaimage, London
Printed and bound by Firmengruppe APPL,
Wemding, Germany

Contents

Introduction

Gardening is one of the best and most fulfilling activities on earth, but it can sometimes seem complicated and confusing. The answers to problems can usually be found in books, but big fat gardening books can be rather daunting. Where do you start? How can you find just the information you want without wading through lots of stuff that is not appropriate to your particular problem? Well, a good index is helpful, but sometimes a smaller book devoted to one particular subject fits the bill better – especially if it is reasonably priced and if you have a small garden where you might not be able to fit in everything suggested in a larger volume.

The *How to Garden* books aim to fill that gap – even if sometimes it may be only a small one. They are clearly set out and written, I hope, in a straightforward, easy-to-understand style. I don't see any point in making gardening complicated, when much of it is based on common sense and observation. (All the key techniques are explained and illustrated, and I've included plenty of tips and tricks of the trade.)

There are suggestions on the best plants and the best varieties to grow in particular situations and for a particular effect. I've tried to keep the information crisp and to the point so that you can find what you need quickly and easily and then put your new-found knowledge into practice. Don't worry if you're not familiar with the Latin names of plants. They are there to make sure you can find the plant as it will be labelled in the nursery or garden centre, but where appropriate I have included common names, too. Forgetting a plant's name need not stand in your way when it comes to being able to grow it.

Above all, the *How to Garden* books are designed to fill you with passion and enthusiasm for your garden and all that its creation and care entails, from designing and planting it to maintaining it and enjoying it. For more than fifty years gardening has been my passion, and that initial enthusiasm for watching plants grow, for trying something new and for just being outside pottering has never faded. If anything I am keener on gardening now than I ever was and get more satisfaction from my plants every day. It's not that I am simply a romantic, but rather that I have learned to look for the good in gardens and in plants, and there is lots to be found. Oh, there are times when I fail – when my plants don't grow as well as they should and I need to try harder. But where would I rather be on a sunny day? Nowhere!

The *How to Garden* handbooks will, I hope, allow some of that enthusiasm – childish though it may be – to rub off on you, and the information they contain will, I hope, make you a better gardener, as well as opening your eyes to the magic of plants and flowers.

Introducing the cutting garden

A traditional cutting garden in the grand country-house style is a rarity today, but the idea of growing your own cut flowers for the house still carries a special magic. A cutting garden can be as tiny as a balcony or as big as the largest garden. It doesn't have to be a separate area – though it can be, of course. But wherever you choose to grow plants to cut for indoors, and on whatever scale, it's important to know which plants will give you the most pleasing effects for the longest time, bearing in mind the space, money and time that you have available.

Why grow plants for cutting?

There can't be many of us who don't love fresh flowers. Having them around us every day is a life-enhancing luxury – but also a very expensive habit if you have to buy them. Growing them at home changes all that, and at the same time adds a new dimension to the garden as well as the house. With a little imaginative planning, even a small plot can produce enough cut flowers and foliage to make a real difference, both for special occasions and as an uplifting part of everyday routine, all through the year.

Even the tiniest arrangement can capture the season – here, primroses and wood anemones in spring.

Variety from the garden

Something different to pick for the house in each week of the year might seem rather ambitious, but it's a good plan to aim for, and in fact a well-stocked garden of reasonable size can do far better than that. We are accustomed to seeing a fairly limited range of traditional florist's flowers, such as chrysanthemums, carnations and alstroemerias, for sale, but such flowers normally have to meet criteria – including a long shelf-life and an ability to travel well – that simply do not apply to garden plants. When it comes to gathering fresh flowers and other plant material from the garden, the choice can be almost limitless if you abandon any preconceived ideas of 'cut flowers' and use a little imagination.

And it's not just flowers …

One of the great joys of growing your own plants for cutting is the tempting variety of different things that you can put together – not only flowers of many shapes and colours, but foliage, berries and seedheads as well. If you bear in mind a few very simple design principles when choosing flowers to grow and pick (*see* pages 14–20), you can enjoy both a beautiful garden and professional-looking indoor arrangements created from a wide choice of fresh plant material, all conveniently available outside your door and costing next to nothing.

The mood of the season

The excitement of picking your first snowdrop of the year, or the thrill of gathering the first bunch of primroses or sweet peas, never seems to diminish. It has no real equivalent in the cut-flower trade, where blooms are often flown in from thousands of miles away, many of them sold all year round. Cutting flowers from your own garden will keep you in touch with the seasons in the most immediate way, and to get to know a succession of plants in the house – like a changing cast of characters through the year – is one of the great pleasures of gardening in general, and of growing for cutting in particular.

A greener option

Recent years have seen aspects of the cut-flower trade coming in for criticism on environmental and ethical grounds. As well as the 'air miles' clocked up by the need for fresh flowers to reach their destination quickly, there is considerable concern about the quantities of chemical pesticides, fungicides and fertilizers used to grow them in other parts of the world, and about the poor working conditions of a great number of people whose livelihood depends on the cut-flower market. Growing your own, as with fruit and vegetables, avoids this whole problematic area: you know exactly where your flowers have come from, who grew them, and what went into their cultivation. And their carbon footprint is not an issue.

Don't forget

Keep a pair of pocket-sized garden snippers by the back door and take them with you to cut a few stems, or even a single flower, whenever you go out. You'll be surprised by what you can find to make a small, original arrangement.

Keeping in touch with your plants

Gathering flowers for the house never quite seems like work. Regular cutting trips help bring the garden into the house through the year, in the most enjoyable of ways. While you're out there you're certain to notice various things you would not otherwise have been aware of, for instance a waft of unexpected fragrance, a family of newly fledged nestlings, or some seasonal flower treasure that has just opened its first bud. Even in poor weather, having a new reason to explore the garden regularly will keep you up to date with all the changing detail of your plants – and it will never, ever feel like a chore.

Florist's flowers are often chosen for their longevity: flowers that last in water for only a day or two are felt to be poor value for money. But with garden flowers you can really spoil yourself, at minimal cost, with fresh bunches every day and almost limitless variety. Some of the loveliest flowers are fleeting, and prevailing weather conditions can affect the life of cut flowers: spring bulbs will complete their growth cycle much faster in warm, dry weather, and late-season flowers brought in from a chilly garden in autumn don't acclimatize well to a warm room and can fade very quickly. But growing your own allows you the luxury of enjoying even the most short-lived flowers at close quarters while they last. Many of your flowers can be given a longer vase life by following the simple advice on page 40.

Don't forget

Invest in a few tiny containers of different shapes and colours. They don't have to be conventional vases – a pretty wine glass or cream jug, or even an elegant jar or bottle work just as well. (See also page 18.)

Plant your garden for variety throughout the year and you'll always find interesting combinations to put together for the house.

Garden specials

There are hundreds of plant treasures that you'll seldom see in florist's shops but which are simplicity itself to grow in the garden and quite special to cut for the house, even if they flower for only a couple of days. Below are a few examples. For more information on garden plants that are suitable for cutting, *see* the A–Z directory, pages 65–91.

SPRING	SUMMER	AUTUMN	WINTER
Convallaria majalis	*Alchemilla mollis*	*Clematis tangutica*	*Chimonanthus praecox*
Iris sibirica	*Catananche caerulea*	*Dipsacus fullonum*	*Cornus alba* cultivars
Lunaria annua	*Eryngium giganteum*	*Humulus lupulus*	*Galanthus nivalis*
Meconopsis cambrica	*Heliotropium arborescens*	*Iris foetidissima*	*Hamamelis × intermedia*
Primula veris	*Lathyrus odoratus*	*Kniphofia*	*Iris unguicularis*
Syringa	*Nigella damascena*	*Physalis alkekengi*	*Jasminum nudiflorum*
Viola odorata	*Paeonia lactiflora*	*Tropaeolum majus*	*Sarcococca confusa*

The compact, pink-flowered lilac *Syringa meyeri* 'Palibin' and purple-flowered *Iris sibirica*.

The generous blooms of *Paeonia lactiflora* with the fluffy lime-green flowers of *Alchemilla mollis*.

The tall spires of red-hot pokers (*Kniphofia rooperi*) and teasels (*Dipsacus fullonum*).

A winter blaze of *Hamamelis × intermedia* 'Ripe Corn' with *Cornus alba* 'Sibirica'.

Less is more

Don't be put off the idea of growing plants for cutting by thinking that you'll need to pick vast quantities of huge blooms at the expense of your garden. Occasionally, of course, it's lovely to splash out and have a large, flamboyant arrangement or a really generous bunch of tulips, but most of the time a spray of flowers put together in your hand is all that's needed. A pretty posy on a window-sill, a carefully selected single bloom or a small jug of fragrant winter flowers will make all the difference to a room, with no noticeable loss to the garden. A well-planned garden will provide inspiration enough, and you'll seldom come back indoors empty-handed.

There's lots to be learned, too. Keep a constant lookout for good combinations of colours, shapes and textures in the garden that would work well in arrangements (and vice versa). Notice what flowers with what. Experiment with putting plants together, and find out, by looking at books and visiting other gardens, which plants share a liking for the same conditions. There is endless scope for creativity, and much satisfaction to be gained from making new discoveries.

Fragrant plants

Often elusive, the scents of garden plants captivate us and linger in the memory. Many plant fragrances begin to fade when flowers are cut and brought indoors – but their initial effect in a room is something really special, and not to be missed. Bring in from the garden whatever you can find that smells nice and enjoy the fragrance while it lasts. For more on fragrant plants for particular seasons, *see* pages 48–62.

What's your style?

Choosing a style of gardening or flower arranging isn't like following a recipe. We all recognize differences between formal and informal, traditional and contemporary and so on, but there are often big overlaps. The best approach is to develop your own unique style based on what broadly appeals to you. In time, you'll soon get to know some of the best plants to grow to achieve the effect you're looking for.

Formal: sophisticated, contemporary, tidy

Not so long ago, formal flower arranging involved time-consuming constructions of perfect, highly bred flowers such as gladioli, Hybrid Tea roses and carnations backed up by a lot of floristry accessories. Now, most of us recognize that isn't really what garden flowers are all about. Instead, home-grown flowers lend themselves to more natural styles of arrangement than many of the manicured, florist's shops blooms. However, it's still possible to 'do' formal from your garden, and to do it well (and a lot more simply).

Contemporary formality can be very straightforward if it is based on strong, simple lines, well-defined shapes and the tightly controlled use of colour. For the crisp effect that is required, it's better not to mix too many different types of flower.

Arrangements need to be easy to 'read', so look to flowers with a stark, clean outline, such as foxtail lily (*Eremurus*), *Allium nigrum*, *Tulipa* 'Queen of Night' or *Acanthus spinosus*. On a smaller scale, *Liriope muscari*, *Veronica gentianoides* and *Muscari botryoides* 'Album' work well to set the style.

An uncomplicated approach suits contemporary spaces, so don't underestimate the effectiveness of a single flower variety used creatively. Experiment with unusually shaped plants and display them almost as if they were sculptures. Try a pair or trio of single stems of an interesting eryngium, each in an elegant bottle; or a tall, slender vase with a few stems of strongly shaped blooms such as alliums, tulips or arum lilies.

Large-scale flowers for grand arrangements

Acanthus spinosus	*Eremurus*
Aruncus dioicus	*Helianthus annuus*
Cephalaria gigantea	*Lilium regale*
Chamaenerion angustifolium 'Album'	*Lupinus*
	Paeonia
Cosmos bipinnatus	*Papaver orientale*
Cynara cardunculus	*Veronicastrum*
Delphinium	*Zantedeschia aethiopica*

Don't forget

For arrangements that lean towards the formal, flowers must be of tip-top quality. Inspect each stem for damage or any shortcomings that might spoil the effect. Condition the flowers if need be (see page 40).

Eremurus have an arresting, sophisticated elegance that brings drama to large arrangements and garden borders alike.

Choose subtle rather than garish colours if a sophisticated effect is what you're after. Understated is best: explore the possibilities of green, cream or 'black' flowers (*see* page 21), and try out the moody, mysterious colours of plants such as *Cerinthe major* 'Purpurascens' or *Nectaroscordum siculum*. Remember that the type of vase you choose will make all the difference: simple, sleek shapes work best, and black or white containers complement cut flowers by their very simplicity. Position your finished arrangement carefully, with a plain, uncluttered background and flattering lighting if possible.

Valuable 'volunteers'

Plants that self-sow help to create a relaxed, informal style of garden and are useful in so many ways. They make a garden look established and comfortable, while lending a sense of coherence and unity. They can work in the same way in arrangements. Some self-sowers make excellent 'filler' plants: a foil for more substantial and distinguished flowers. And, of course, they're free! Try the following and see what will enjoy your soil and site.

Aquilegia

Centranthus ruber

Digitalis purpurea

Eryngium giganteum

Hesperis matronalis

Lunaria annua var. *albiflora* 'Alba Variegata'

Lychnis coronaria

Meconopsis cambrica

Myosotis sylvatica

Nicandra physalodes

Nigella damascena

Papaver somniferum

The deep-crimson cultivated thistle *Cirsium rivulare* 'Atropurpureum', seen here with hardy geraniums and a rambling rose, is invaluable for lending an informal touch.

Informal: romantic, natural, rustic

Simple, traditional country flowers are hard to beat, and look perfectly at home in many different kinds of surroundings. 'Natural' flower arrangements using time-honoured favourites, for instance wallflowers, sweet peas and lily-of-the-valley, have become a lot more popular in recent years. It is now quite usual, even for formal occasions such as weddings, to see arrangements using cottage-garden plants and sometimes wildflowers too. This is good news for the cutting garden: no more manicuring or spraying to achieve the perfect rose or chrysanthemum bloom. Instead, more or less anything goes, provided it is creatively put together for a beautiful result that appears to have been effortless.

A bunch of country-style flowers must above all look as fresh as possible. Generous use of green and white, with some blue perhaps, will not only help to give that effect but will also work well as a frame for a mixture of other flowers, lending coherence and preventing clashes. Arrange a simple bunch of flowers as you walk round the garden. Select a mixture of sizes and don't overlook the 'everyday' plants such as *Tellima grandiflora* or *Alchemilla mollis*. And remember to use grasses and their ilk: the delicate flowerheads of the quaking grass *Briza maxima* or woodrush (*Luzula sylvatica*) are very long-lasting and can set off an informal arrangement to perfection.

Design principles

With tens of thousands of plants to choose from, there are limitless possibilities for partnerships and groupings. It can be hard to know where to begin. But whether you're putting plants together in a garden bed or in a vase, it's helpful to be aware of the essential properties of each plant such as shape, texture and colour. Get to know how these work, and learn a few basic techniques that help them to interact with each other to produce the most satisfying results.

Opposites attract: the poppy *Papaver orientale* 'Patty's Plum' is set off to perfection by *Euphorbia* and *Cerinthe*.

Flower and foliage shapes

A garden border that is to look interesting throughout the year needs plants and flowers of different shapes, preferably arranged in such a way as to lead the eye through what might otherwise appear to be a confusing muddle. A good balance of plant, leaf and flower shapes is at least as important as colour when you're designing a permanent border – both for the appearance of the border itself and to give you a wide choice of material for cutting.

Upright shapes

Vertical plants are important as punctuation marks in planting schemes, and repeating such plants immediately lends a strong sense of coherence to a bed or border, as well as emphasizing the all-important third dimension, height. In a bigger bed, the larger verticals might take the form of fastigiate shrubs such as upright forms of yew, common juniper or purple-leaved berberis – all of which can provide a certain amount of usable foliage for flower arrangements, provided you cut it carefully so as not to spoil the shape of the bush. In a small space, the upright components might take the form of a compact kniphofia, salvia or veronica to provide flower spikes for cutting, or plants with sword-shaped leaves such as irises, sisyrinchiums or certain grasses.

'Drumstick' flowers are also useful to add height and strong shapes. Alliums are a good choice, with varieties in many different sizes and colours, but also worth considering are tulips, globe thistles (*Echinops*), cultivars of agapanthus and the globular seedheads of opium poppies (*Papaver somniferum*).

Apart from their visual effects, many upright plants have stiff stems that act as useful 'scaffolding' in arrangements, helping to hold other plants in place (*see* page 20).

Stiff, straight vertical spikes, such as those of red-hot pokers (*Kniphofia*), are important for structure and height.

Flat shapes

The strong, positive shapes of dominant vertical garden plants will tend to be highlighted by giving them contrasting companions. These might be some of the many different kinds of euphorbia and other perennials with flat plates of flowers that create horizontal pools of colour: achilleas and sedums both contribute useful and long-lasting structural effects in the garden as their colour slowly recedes to leave durable brown and russet seedheads, useful for cutting in autumn and winter. Daisy-type flowers offer a

The bold, flat discs and clear, simple colours of daisies make most of them excellent partners for a great variety of other cut flowers.

Easy and long-lasting, the flattened domed flowerheads of tall sedums such as 'Herbstfreude' give horizontal structure of a different kind.

Don't forget

Although it's great to have a good variety of plants for cutting, avoid the 'one-of-each' approach. Both in borders and in arrangements, some key plants should be repeated if you are to avoid a random, spotty effect.

different type of contrast. Try to include some of these, such as anthemis, echinaceas, rudbeckias or the simple yet pretty ox-eye daisy *Leucanthemum vulgare*, which will

make itself at home in any odd corner and flowers for months provided it is dead-headed. It is worth establishing in an area of informal long grass.

Good mixers

While some plants make a special feature in a vase on their own, others (listed below) belong in the supporting cast, as plants to mix with grander flowers.

Achillea ptarmica

Alchemilla mollis

Allium tuberosum

Anthemis tinctoria 'Sauce Hollandaise'

Astrantia major 'Sunningdale Variegated'

Bupleurum falcatum

Centranthus ruber 'Albus'

Euphorbia amygdaloides var. *robbiae*

Euphorbia cyparissias 'Fens Ruby'

Galium odoratum

Gypsophila paniculata

Strong vertical and horizontal plants work wonders, either together or separately, as visual support for less well-defined shapes.

This uplifting mix of two contrasting colour groups with a backdrop of green foliage would look just as effective in a vase.

Planning for colour

Whole books have been devoted to the subject of colour in the garden, recommending dos and don'ts of all kinds. Often, these recommend limiting the colour palette to just a few colours to produce satisfying schemes. However, when you're planting garden beds and borders with cutting in mind you need to take a more relaxed approach, as being over-restrictive with colour schemes can leave you with too limited a choice of plant material.

If you grow a wide range of colours together and want to prevent unwelcome clashes, using plenty of green is the answer. Warring colours in gardens are most obvious where green is in short supply – think of yellow forsythia and pink flowering currant (*Ribes*)

blooming together in spring before their leaves are fully open.

Other neutral colours, such as whites, creams and blues, will also help to dilute clashing colours, and work in both vases and the garden. The same applies to plants with silver leaves, which brighten up the garden and can give a huge lift to a bunch of flowers in deep, jewel-like reds and blues.

Seasonal combinations

The prevailing colours of different seasons are also worth bearing in mind when you're choosing plants

An unusual spring partnership of rich colours: *Tulipa* 'Queen of Night' with the prickly arching shrub *Rubus cockburnianus* 'Goldenvale'.

to put together in the garden. In spring, for example, you can't beat the freshness of blues, white and yellow, which mostly go well together – especially with plenty of new greenery – whether in borders or when cut for the house. Strong colours such as red and orange can either be confined to a cutting bed in a separate part of the garden, or saved for later in the year, when the low light of late summer is especially flattering to them.

Stark contrasts in both shape and colour make this juxtaposition of blue delphiniums and bright yellow achilleas an arresting combination.

Create excitement with daring contrasts such as blue and orange: here, California poppies with moody dark blue cerinthe.

Harmonious colour schemes demand contrasting shapes or textures. Dainty *Astrantia* 'Roma' here partners bold *Allium cristophii*.

Planning for contrast

Contrast, of one sort or another, is part of the magic formula for most successful partnerships in the garden or in mixed arrangements. Strongly structural plants and soft, fluffy ones bring out the best in each other, as do contrasting colours such as red and green, dark blue and white, or orange and deep violet. A good starting point when you are putting plants together is to check that you have at least two pairs of contrasting features, which might be colour, shape or texture.

Contrasts and harmonies

The impact of any particular colour varies greatly according to a number of factors, including light, weather, time of day (or year) and – most important in flower arranging – the colours that surround it. To create maximum impact, juxtapose one colour with another that is a strong contrast: red with green, violet-blue with orange or blue with yellow.

Balance the proportions carefully, though. Very often, a small amount of a contrasting colour is more effective than equal proportions and is just right to give a 'lift' to the whole scheme, whether it's a flower bed or a bunch of cut flowers. To see how this works, try adding three or five white or cream-coloured flowers to a bouquet in rich, dark colours, or boost a scheme of greens and blues with just a few pinpoints of bright red.

Although harmonious colour schemes can be somewhat limiting in a cutting garden, there will be times when you will want to create arrangements using single colours or close harmonies. Pastel shades belong together and combine well with deeper blues but not usually with 'hot' colours like orange, bright yellow and scarlet. But the saturation of a colour can make a difference to its suitability as a partner: pastel yellow and deep pink can work very well, for example, where bright yellow and soft pink do not.

Tulips and wallflowers are a classic spring partnership. Here, *Tulipa* 'Ballerina' harmonizes with *Erysimum cheiri* 'Fire King'.

In this late-summer pairing, the long tassels of *Itea ilicifolia* give a welcome lift to the lacecap *Hydrangea aspera* Villosa Group.

Vases, jugs and bowls

Flowers can look great in the most unlikely containers, and you're sure to have your own favourites. It's a good idea to have a range of basic containers that will complement the colours and styles of a wide variety of plants. Flea markets and antique shops are fun places to hunt for interesting jugs, vases and bowls – they don't have to be made for flowers. Simple shapes and colours are usually best, so as not to overpower their contents, as patterns can easily do. White works well with fresh-looking spring arrangements, black or dark blue with bright, hot colours or acid greens; silver, pewter or brass with blues or pastel shades. Simple terracotta tends to be flattering to blues and greens.

Jugs and vases

These can be among the most useful flower containers – small ones are the easiest to store. At almost any time of year, miniature vases, especially ones with a narrow neck, are handy for a few stems of small plants such as snowdrops or forget-me-nots, sprigs of fragrant daphne or sarcococca, lavender, lily-of-the-valley or individual clematis flowers. Partner these with a sprig or two of small-leaved foliage in a pretty white or silver jug or a small blue glass, and you immediately have something to transform a windowsill, a desk or a bedside table.

A narrow-necked container to hold a tulip, rose, allium or other single bloom is ideal for a small table or desk, giving the chance to look closely at a flower without taking a whole bunch from the garden. An elegantly shaped bottle might do the trick, or select a vase that is bulbous at the base. Make sure whatever you choose will not be top-heavy once it has a flower in it.

Generous bunches of daffodils or tulips need a larger container that will support the stems while allowing the flowers to look natural and uncontrived; a plain ceramic jug, narrower at the top than at the base, is just right.

Bright flowers with long, straight stems, such as alliums and some types of iris, look elegant in a tall, dark-coloured vase if you have a suitable place to display them. Again, make sure that the arrangement will not be top-heavy. Marbles or stones in the base of the container may help.

Bowls

Rounded bowls, with or without pin-holders or florist's foam, are useful for dome-shaped arrangements of shorter-stemmed flowers. Use bushy foliage or frothy flowers such as *Alchemilla mollis* as a base and background for stronger shapes and colours. Very shallow bowls or plates, especially those in dark colours, can be

The right container makes a big difference to the finished effect.

① A simple ceramic jug is just the thing for a bunch of country flowers.

② Pretty glass bottles work well, singly or grouped, for one or two stems, like these *Anemone coronaria*.

③ Hellebore flowers show up better and last longer in a flat, shallow container.

used to float the flowerheads of hellebores (*see* above), pansies or dahlias in shallow water so that their 'faces' are framed and displayed to best effect.

Don't forget

Some flowers, including snowdrops, discolour the water in their container, while others have unattractive stems that begin to turn yellow in water. For these, use a ceramic or other opaque vase instead of one made of clear glass.

Pennisetums are among the fluffiest grasses but many are tender, including *Pennisetum setaceum*, shown here with *Verbena bonariensis*.

Gypsophila has long been valued by florists as a useful 'filler' plant. Here, its tiny white flowers combine prettily with *Scabiosa caucasica*.

Contrasting colour and texture using annuals: white, lacy *Ammi majus* combined with the dark flowerheads of *Scabiosa atropurpurea*.

Textures

Combining plants with different textures, whether within the garden or in arrangements, is a whole aspect of being creative with plants and is well worth exploring. Leaves, for example, can be leathery, spiny or furry; flowers waxy, fluffy, frilly or silky; seedpods papery, bristly or bobbly. Start to notice the characteristics of your plants at different times of the year and experiment with putting them together in borders and vases to make interesting combinations.

Important in the garden as a foil for more strongly structured plants are flowers and foliage with a soft texture and airy habit that helps them diffuse light. They are just as effective in giving a softer edge to cut-flower arrangements. Gypsophila is a popular florist's choice for this role, as is asparagus fern (*Asparagus setaceus*). You can grow both of

these in the garden. Feathery grasses are also very useful for providing texture, including the fluffy bottlebrushes of *Pennisetum villosum* and *Pennisetum setaceum*. Very fine, silky grasses, such as *Stipa tenuissima*, don't work so well in a vase.

Don't overlook other, less well-known plants that have the same open texture. Wild umbellifers, for example cow parsley, look good for a while, although most soon shed their tiny petals. Cultivated plants of this type with white petals include *Ammi majus* and *Orlaya grandiflora*. *Chaerophyllum hirsutum* 'Roseum' and *Pimpinella major* 'Rosea' offer a similar effect in pink; *Limonium platyphyllum* in soft violet; and don't forget the light-as-air, tiny lime-green flowers of *Alchemilla mollis*, which enhance almost anything that you put them with.

On a smaller scale are sweet woodruff (*Galium odoratum*), a

woodland carpeter with umbels of tiny white flowers that are extremely handy for any petite arrangement, and the easy, shade-loving *Saxifraga × urbium*, with dainty pale pink flowers arranged on longer stems.

Colour harmony with textural contrast: *Euonymus fortunei* 'Emerald 'n' Gold' with the grass *Hakonechloa macra* 'Aureola'.

Eryngium giganteum is a particularly useful framework plant, with its distinctive prickles and branching stems forming a strong support structure.

Framework plants

A framework or bone structure in an arrangement of cut flowers and foliage is not only visually satisfying, it also performs the practical role of helping to keep everything together without the need for floristry accessories such as wire and florist's foam. Choosing the right materials for this key task is an important first step, so include in your garden scheme a good range of long-lasting structural plants. Many of them are easy to grow and contribute just as much to the garden as they will to your flower arrangements. Eryngiums, for example, will provide stiff stems and intricate silver or steely-blue flowers for several weeks in summer, while bare twigs cut from the coloured stems of an ornamental dogwood such as *Cornus alba* 'Sibirica Variegata' make an effective framework for autumn and winter arrangements. A few flowerheads of *Alchemilla mollis*, fennel or euphorbia make a good starting point for a mixed bunch, both providing a flattering backdrop for other flowers and helping to hold them in place.

Love-in-a-mist (*Nigella damascena*) has rigid, wiry stems and pliable, feathery leaves to support and complement other plants (here, *Moluccella laevis*).

Stiff fennel flowerheads are invaluable late-summer vase companions. Here their partner is the neat but robust and prolific *Dahlia* 'David Howard'.

Good framework plants

Alchemilla mollis

Aster lateriflorus var. *horizontalis*

Buxus sempervirens

Cornus alba

Dipsacus fullonum

Eryngium giganteum

Foeniculum vulgare (flowerheads)

Hebe rakaiensis

Ilex aquifolium

Nigella damascena

Origanum

Osmanthus delavayi

Phlomis

Pittosporum tenuifolium

Rhamnus alaternus 'Argenteovariegata'

Rosmarinus officinalis

Santolina

Tellima grandiflora

Verbena bonariensis

Design palette

These lists should help you to narrow down the endless range of possibilities when you're choosing plants for particular visual effects. *See also* the A–Z directory, pages 65–91.

Flower colour

GREEN FLOWERS

Alchemilla mollis
Eucomis bicolor
Euphorbia amygdaloides var. *robbiae*
Heuchera cylindrica 'Greenfinch'
Moluccella laevis
Nicotiana 'Lime Green' (right)
Skimmia × confusa 'Kew Green'
Tellima grandiflora
Tulipa 'Spring Green'
Zinnia 'Envy'

RED FLOWERS

Anemone pavonina (right)
Crocosmia 'Lucifer'
Dahlia 'Bishop of Llandaff'
Geum 'Mrs J. Bradshaw'
Lychnis chalcedonica
Paeonia 'Buckeye Belle'
Persicaria amplexicaulis 'Taurus'
Potentilla 'Gibson's Scarlet'
Salvia fulgens
Tulipa 'Couleur Cardinal'

ORANGE FLOWERS

Achillea 'Terracotta'
Alstroemeria
Crocosmia 'Zambesi'
Erysimum 'Apricot Twist'
Euphorbia griffithii 'Fireglow'
Gaillardia 'Oranges and Lemons'
Geum 'Prinses Juliana' (right)
Helenium 'Sahin's Early Flowerer'
Kniphofia rooperi
Tulipa 'Prinses Irene'

PINK AND MAUVE FLOWERS

Dianthus barbatus
Echinacea purpurea (right)
Heliotropium arborescens
Lathyrus odoratus
Paeonia lactiflora 'Sarah Bernhardt'
Pimpinella major 'Rosea'
Polemonium 'Lambrook Mauve'
Rosa 'Gertrude Jekyll'
Tulipa 'China Pink'

BLUE AND VIOLET FLOWERS

Agapanthus 'Lilliput' (right)
Aquilegia alpina
Campanula
Consolida ajacis
Eryngium alpinum
Lavandula angustifolia 'Imperial Gem'
Nigella damascena
Perovskia atriplicifolia
Pulmonaria 'Blue Ensign'
Veronica

YELLOW FLOWERS

Allium moly
Coreopsis verticillata
Doronicum orientale (right)
Helenium 'Butterpat'
Helianthus 'Lemon Queen'
Narcissus 'Tête-à-Tête'
Primula vulgaris
Rosa 'Graham Thomas'
Rudbeckia laciniata 'Herbstsonne'
Tulipa 'West Point'

WHITE AND CREAM FLOWERS

Anemone × hybrida 'Honorine Jobert'
Aruncus dioicus (right)
Galanthus 'Atkinsii'
Kniphofia 'Little Maid'
Lilium regale
Muscari botryoides 'Album'
Narcissus 'Thalia'
Orlaya grandiflora
Phlox paniculata 'Mount Fuji'
Zantedeschia aethiopica

BLACK AND PURPLE FLOWERS

Centaurea cyanus 'Black Ball'
Iris 'Superstition' (right)
Iris tuberosa
Nicandra physalodes
Penstemon 'Raven'
Rudbeckia occidentalis 'Green Wizard'
Scabiosa atropurpurea 'Chile Black'
Tulipa 'Queen of Night'
Viola 'Molly Sanderson'

Flower shape

VERTICAL SPIKES

Delphinium
Digitalis
Eremurus (right)
Kniphofia
Lavandula angustifolia
Liriope muscari
Lupinus
Lysimachia clethroides
Nepeta
Veronica
Veronicastrum

HORIZONTAL DISCS/DOMES

Achillea
Anthemis
Doronicum orientale
Euphorbia
Helenium
Orlaya grandiflora (right)
Phlomis russeliana
Pimpinella major 'Rosea'
Rudbeckia
Scabiosa caucasica 'Clive Greaves'
Sedum 'Herbstfreude'

PENDENT/ARCHING

Briza maxima
Carex pendula
Chasmanthium latifolium
Convallaria majalis
Dierama pulcherrimum
Fuchsia
Galanthus 'Magnet'
Geum rivale 'Leonard's Variety'
Lamprocapnos spectabilis (right)
Leucojum vernum
Polygonatum × hybridum

DRUMSTICKS

Agapanthus
Allium hollandicum
Allium neapolitanum
Allium schoenoprasum
Allium sphaerocephalon
Armeria maritima
Cirsium rivulare 'Atropurpureum'
Echinops ritro 'Veitch's Blue'
Muscari botryoides 'Album'
Primula denticulata
Tulipa 'Queen of Night' (right)

Foliage colour

GOLDEN FOLIAGE

Choisya ternata 'Sundance'
Cornus alba 'Spaethii'
Hedera helix 'Buttercup' (right)
Humulus lupulus 'Aureus'
Lamium maculatum 'Aureum'
Lonicera nitida 'Baggesen's Gold'
Origanum vulgare 'Aureum'
Osmanthus heterophyllus 'Goshiki'
Physocarpus opulifolius 'Dart's Gold'
Tanacetum parthenium 'Aureum'
Taxus baccata Aurea Group

VARIEGATED FOLIAGE

Arum italicum 'Marmoratum' (right)
Buxus sempervirens 'Elegantissima'
Cornus alba 'Sibirica Variegata'
Eryngium bourgatii
Euonymus fortunei 'Silver Queen'
Hedera helix 'Glacier'
Hosta 'Ginko Craig'
Luma apiculata 'Glanleam Gold'
Pittosporum 'Garnettii'
Pulmonaria 'Lewis Palmer'
Rhamnus alaternus 'Argenteovariegata'

BRONZE/PURPLE FOLIAGE

Berberis thunbergii 'Helmond Pillar'
Corylus maxima 'Purpurea'
Cotinus coggygria 'Royal Purple'
Fagus sylvatica 'Dawyck Purple'
Foeniculum vulgare 'Purpureum'
Geranium phaeum 'Samobor'
Hebe 'Mrs Winder'
Heuchera 'Obsidian' (right)
Osmanthus heterophyllus 'Purpureus'
Pittosporum tenuifolium 'Purpureum'
Sambucus nigra 'Eva'

SILVER FOLIAGE

Artemisia ludoviciana 'Valerie Finnis'
Atriplex halimus
Convolvulus cneorum
Elaeagnus 'Quicksilver'
Eucalyptus gunnii
Helichrysum italicum 'Korma'
Hippophae rhamnoides
Olea europaea
Pulmonaria 'Majesté' (right)
Pyrus salicifolia 'Pendula'
Salix exigua

Other ornamental features

COLOURED STEMS

Acer palmatum 'Sango-kaku' (right)
Cornus alba 'Elegantissima'
Cornus alba 'Kesselringii'
Cornus sanguinea 'Midwinter Fire'
Cornus sericea 'Flaviramea'
Eryngium × oliverianum
Kerria japonica 'Pleniflora'
Phyllostachys nigra
Rubus thibetanus
Salix alba var. vitellina 'Britzensis'
Salix daphnoides 'Aglaia'

INTERESTING SEEDHEADS

Allium cristophii
Clematis tangutica (right)
Crocosmia (some)
Dipsacus fullonum
Eryngium giganteum
Lunaria annua
Nicandra physalodes
Papaver somniferum
Phlomis russeliana
Physalis alkekengi
Tulipa turkestanica

CATKINS AND BUDS

Acer davidii
Aesculus hippocastanum
Alnus incana 'Aurea'
Betula pendula
Corylus avellana
Larix decidua
Magnolia stellata
Salix caprea (right)
Salix gracilistyla 'Melanostachys'
Skimmia japonica 'Rubella'
Viburnum tinus

ORNAMENTAL FRUITS

Callicarpa bodinieri 'Profusion'
Cotoneaster
Euonymus planipes
Hedera helix
Ilex aquifolium
Iris foetidissima
Myrtus communis
Ophiopogon planiscapus 'Nigrescens'
Rosa 'Geranium' (right)
Viburnum davidii
Viburnum opulus

Mood and style

VIBRANT AND DRAMATIC

Aster 'Little Carlow'
Crocosmia 'Lucifer'
Delphinium Black Knight Group
Echinacea purpurea 'Fatal Attraction'
Lobelia × speciosa 'Tania'
Paeonia 'Buckeye Belle' (right)
Rosa 'William Shakespeare 2000'
Rudbeckia laciniata 'Herbstsonne'
Salvia × superba
Tulipa 'Queen of Sheba'
Zinnia

CALM AND SUBTLE

Catananche caerulea
Clematis 'Betty Corning'
Geranium clarkei 'Kashmir White'
Gypsophila 'Rosenschleier'
Malva moschata
Muscari armeniacum 'Valerie Finnis'
Penstemon 'Evelyn'
Pulmonaria 'Opal'
Rosa 'New Dawn' (right)
Tulipa 'Sapporo'
Vinca difformis

BOLD AND ARCHITECTURAL

Acanthus spinosus
Achillea filipendulina 'Gold Plate'
Agapanthus 'Jack's Blue'
Allium 'Globemaster'
Crocosmia 'Lucifer'
Cynara cardunculus (right)
Delphinium 'Alice Artindale'
Helianthus annuus
Hydrangea paniculata 'Grandiflora'
Lilium regale
Zantedeschia aethiopica

DAINTY AND DELICATE

Alchemilla mollis
Dianthus deltoides
Epimedium
Erigeron karvinskianus
Eryngium × tripartitum
Galium odoratum
Gypsophila
Heuchera
Myosotis (right)
Saxifraga × urbium
Viola sororia 'Freckles'

Planning your cutting garden

Unless you have an enormous garden, value for space will be an important consideration when you're planning for cut flowers. You'll want to have a succession of flowers and other plant material – foliage, berries and seedheads – to give you interest and beauty all through the year, and you'll want to gather flowers for the house without the garden looking any the worse for it. A tall order? Not if you plan and choose carefully at the outset, so that each plant can do its very best for you.

The first decision to make when you begin to focus on growing flowers for cutting is whether to make a designated cutting bed or to adapt your existing borders, by adding plants that will produce good cutting material and perhaps by growing larger clumps so that flowers and foliage can be picked without making the border look depleted.

A cutting bed

Devoting a whole bed or an area specifically to cut flowers for the house is a lovely idea, whether it's incorporated into a vegetable plot or allotment, or is an ornamental feature in its own right. Whatever the size of your garden, a well-tended cutting bed can be a real asset to both garden and house. It will be more of a commitment, both to plan and to look after, but if you're keen to have large flowers of top quality, it is probably a better option than relying on mixed borders, especially if you prefer to use large numbers of a single variety.

Planning and preparation

A cutting garden or cutting bed can be as ambitious or as simple as you

Rustic screening, hazel wigwams and a neat edging of box help to impose a sense of order on cutting beds that might otherwise look untidy by midsummer.

like. A geometric layout of several meticulously planned and generously planted beds can look wonderful and is sure to inspire the florist in you, but it can be just as rewarding to put together attractive mixtures of flowers chosen from a tiny but creatively designed bed.

Choose a position that is fairly level, sheltered, sunny and well drained. Try to plan your bed or beds so you won't have to walk on the cultivated area to gather flowers. In practice, this is likely to mean a maximum width of 1.2m (4ft), so that you can reach the middle of the bed from an adjacent path.

Some kind of edging is a good idea, both to give a neat finish and to help prevent plants flopping onto the path. The edging could form part of your cutting garden if you create it from lavender, santolina or some similarly compact, bushy plant, or it could take the form of a low

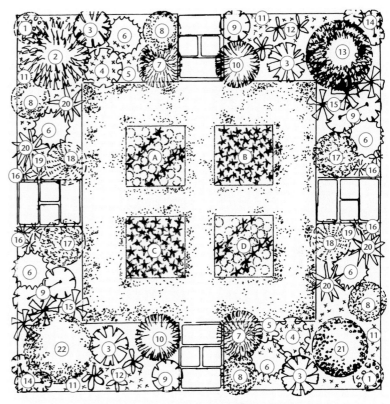

Growing cut flowers on an allotment

Allotments aren't only for vegetables. The bye-laws of some allotment sites may prohibit permanent planting, but annuals are usually fine. Nasturtiums, cosmos, pot marigolds (*Calendula*), *Ammi majus* and, of course, sweet peas all lend themselves to being grown in rows, given suitable support. Other annuals such as poached-egg flower (*Limnanthes douglasii*) and French marigolds (*Tagetes*) are popular as companion plants for their effect in encouraging beneficial predators or deterring pests. You may fancy following the time-honoured allotment tradition of growing outsize dahlias, gladioli and chrysanthemums for cutting. And don't forget spring bulbs. Rows of narcissi, tulips and alliums provide welcome early-season inspiration as well as flowers to bring home. Remember to take a bucket so you can keep the flowers in a little water for their journey home.

1 *Euphorbia amygdaloides* var. *robbiae* (× 2)
2 *Osmanthus heterophyllus* 'Variegatus' (× 1)
3 *Salvia* × *superba* 'Superba' (× 4)
4 *Dahlia* 'Bishop of Llandaff' (× 2)
5 *Anemone coronaria* (× 60)
6 *Eryngium giganteum* (× 6)
7 *Hyssopus officinalis* (× 2)
8 *Alchemilla mollis* (× 4)
9 *Heuchera* 'Obsidian' (× 6)
10 *Lavandula angustifolia* 'Imperial Gem' (× 2)
11 *Narcissus* 'Jack Snipe' (× 60)
12 *Digitalis lutea* (× 6)
13 *Sarcococca confusa* (× 1)
14 *Tellima grandiflora* (× 6)
15 *Lilium regale* (× 6)
16 *Ophiopogon planiscapus* 'Nigrescens' (× 4)

17 *Limonium platyphyllum* (× 2)
18 *Perovskia atriplicifolia* 'Little Spire' (× 2)
19 *Galanthus* 'S. Arnott' (× 20)
20 *Crocosmia* 'Lucifer' (× 4)
21 *Pittosporum tenuifolium* 'Tom Thumb' (× 1)
22 *Buxus sempervirens* 'Elegantissima' (× 1)

Beds A and D:

Spring: *Allium cristophii* (× 50) with *Tulipa turkestanica* (× 50)

Summer annuals from seed: *Nigella hispanica* with *Calendula officinalis*

Beds B and C:

Spring: *Tulipa* 'Prinses Irene' (× 50), 'Queen of Night' (× 50), 'Sapporo' (× 50)

Summer annuals from seed: *Tropaeolum majus* 'Empress of India' with *Cerinthe major* 'Purpurascens'

A SUNNY CUTTING GARDEN (5M/16FT × 5M/16FT)
There is a 90cm (3ft) border round the outside of this garden, so there is no need to tread on the soil while picking flowers and foliage. The mix of shrubs, perennials and bulbs gives a choice of cutting material at every season. The central gravelled area has easily accessible beds that can be planted with bulbs and bedding each year.

1 *Elaeagnus* 'Quicksilver' (× 1)
2 *Clematis* × *durandii* (× 2) (one trained through *Elaeagnus*, the other on obelisk)
3 *Pulmonaria* 'Diana Clare' (× 7)
4 *Galanthus* 'Magnet' (× 30)
5 *Cyclamen coum* (× 20)
6 *Narcissus* 'Ice Wings' (× 60)
7 *Polemonium* 'Lambrook Mauve' (× 2)
8 *Verbena bonariensis* (× 6)
9 *Eryngium bourgatii* (× 7)

10 *Sedum* Herbstfreude Group 'Herbstfreude' (× 3)
11 *Catananche caerulea* (× 8)
12 *Knautia macedonica* (× 5)
13 *Luma apiculata* 'Glanleam Gold' (× 1)
14 *Chionodoxa luciliae* (× 150) (between stepping stones)
15 *Cosmos bipinnatus* (× 3)
16 *Dipsacus fullonum* (× 4)
17 *Nepeta* 'Six Hills Giant' (× 2)
18 *Tulipa* 'China Pink' (× 60)

19 *Echinops ritro* 'Veitch's Blue' (× 2)
20 *Erysimum* 'Bowles's Mauve' (× 1)
21 *Sambucus nigra* 'Eva' (× 1)
22 *Euphorbia schillingii* (× 3)
23 *Lathyrus odoratus* (trained on obelisks) (× 15)
24 *Lunaria annua* (× 2)
25 *Allium sphaerocephalon* (× 60)
26 *Rosmarinus officinalis* 'Miss Jessopp's Upright' (× 1)

A SUNNY MIXED BORDER TO INCLUDE PLANTS FOR CUTTING ALL YEAR ROUND (7M/23FT x 2.5M/8FT)
Planted with a wide range of cutting material from early-spring bulbs through summer annuals and perennials to autumn and winter seedheads, this border is always full of interest. Shrubs (including two evergreens) provide a variety of foliage for cutting, and three obelisks support sweet peas and a clematis. An unobtrusive, informal path of stepping stones threads through the border to allow access for gathering the flowers and foliage.

fence or wall, either temporary or built as a permanent feature.

Prepare the soil as you would for a vegetable garden. Dig it deeply to promote the healthy root growth that will help you produce the maximum harvest from minimum space. Be particularly careful to remove any perennial weeds, and add plenty of well-rotted compost to help prevent the soil drying out.

A mixed border

There's no reason at all not to grow flowers for cutting in your borders rather than in a purpose-made cutting garden. In fact, in a garden of reasonable size, this can be a better use of space. An integrated planting scheme using shrubs and perennials as well as bulbs and annuals will also give you a wider range of cutting material to choose from throughout the year. You'll have plenty of foliage to use in mixed arrangements, too. With careful planning, there won't be many days in the year when you can't find at least something to put in a vase, from a few sprigs of fragrant blossom in late winter to an autumn arrangement of dramatic seedheads and colourful berries.

Mixed borders give great opportunities for space-saving layered planting, where climbers

Don't forget

A densely packed, mixed border needn't be difficult to maintain, provided you have chosen the right plants for your particular situation (see pages 30–2). See pages 42–3 for when and how to carry out an annual overhaul.

can scramble up through shrubs and provide strands of honeysuckle (*Lonicera*) or richly coloured clematis flowers to pick. Spring-flowering bulbs can happily be tucked under deciduous shrubs and among perennials, and will largely look after themselves and multiply, providing enough flowers for the house without noticeably detracting from the garden.

Annuals and biennials that tend to perpetuate themselves by self-sowing from year to year are another trouble-free bonus in mixed schemes, often choosing convenient spots to fill gaps among perennials and shrubs, and lending coherence to the whole garden. Many of these plants are especially valuable for cutting – honesty (*Lunaria annua*), *Eryngium giganteum*, *Verbena bonariensis* and love-in-a-mist (*Nigella damascena*) to name a few. Learn to recognize their seedlings even when they are tiny, and look out for them when weeding, so you can avoid the ones you'd like to keep. For more on self-sowers, see box, page 13.

Tiny gardens

Even a very small garden can make a valuable contribution to indoor arrangements if you choose plants that earn their space. Combine a few hard-working, year-round plants of different types with some eye-catching seasonal highlights. Spring bulbs are especially good space-savers because they can share their patch with later-flowering perennials, some of which (such as eryngiums and sedums) will produce both summer flowers and attractive seedheads for autumn and winter use. And don't forget the huge potential of climbers in small areas. Clematis, honeysuckle, sweet peas, nasturtiums and roses are among those that can produce abundant cut flowers from very little ground space.

Using containers

If your garden consists of a balcony, roof garden, courtyard or other confined area with little or no soil, you may want to make a cutting garden in containers. Buy some of the largest size possible and plan for a good succession of mixed plants to cut for small arrangements, using layered planting in much the same way as in a mixed border but on a smaller scale. A few single specimen shrubs might include *Sarcococca confusa*, for winter greenery and scent, a compact pittosporum and a witch hazel (*Hamamelis mollis*) or *Magnolia stellata* underplanted with bulbs. Sweet peas can provide a bumper cutting harvest in summer if planted in a large container in a sunny spot and kept well watered. Cosmos, phygelius and marguerite (*Argyranthemum frutescens*) will also give a reasonable yield of cut flowers from pots: in each case, it is best to establish a single, healthy, well-grown specimen, which will respond generously to cutting by producing more flowers.

Bulbs can also be planted in attractive smaller pots for taking into the house intact as the flowers are opening; they will last longer than if they are cut, and may be reusable in subsequent years, either still in their pots or planted out. In the same way, other plants such as lily-of-the-valley, ferns, variegated ivies and grasses like *Hakonechloa* will all make pleasing pot plants in a cool room for a while before being returned to their permanent home outdoors. For more tolerance of warmth and sunshine or central heating, try sempervivums, agaves or astelias.

A cutting garden in less than a year

Worthwhile results in the garden can sometimes seem slow to arrive. When you're eagerly waiting to gather your first crop of cut flowers, it's encouraging if you can see the fruits of your labours without too long a wait. A well-chosen mixture of bulbs, bedding plants and seeds will give your cutting garden a flying start, with masses of flowers for the house all through the first spring and summer. Autumn is the best time to start, preparing the soil and putting in bulbs, perennials and spring bedding; the following spring, sow seeds of summer-flowering plants.

AUTUMN PLANTING, SPRING FLOWERING:	AUTUMN SOWING OR PLANTING, SUMMER FLOWERING:	SPRING SOWING OR PLANTING, SUMMER FLOWERING:
Allium hollandicum	*Allium sphaerocephalon*	*Briza maxima*
Anemone coronaria	*Alchemilla mollis*	*Calendula officinalis*
Erysimum cheiri	*Cerinthe major* 'Purpurascens'	*Centaurea cyanus* 'Black Ball'
Galanthus 'Magnet'	*Dianthus barbatus*	*Consolida ajacis*
Hyacinthus orientalis 'Blue Pearl'	*Eryngium alpinum*	*Cosmos bipinnatus*
Muscari aucheri 'White Magic'	*Iris latifolia*	*Dahlia* 'Arabian Night'
Myosotis	*Lathyrus odoratus*	*Galtonia candicans*
Narcissus 'Thalia'	*Lilium regale*	*Gladiolus* × *colvillii* 'The Bride'
Narcissus 'Tête-à-tête'	*Nigella damascena*	*Gypsophila elegans*
Tulipa 'Ballerina'	*Triteleia laxa* 'Koningin Fabiola'	*Matthiola incana*
Tulipa praestans 'Fusilier'		*Salvia viridis*
Tulipa 'Sapporo'		*Zinnia*

Planting and growing

Much of the fascination of growing and using cut flowers and foliage lies in experimenting and making your own discoveries. It's fun to try out different plants, and to find imaginative and satisfying ways of putting them together. Trial and error make life interesting, but when it comes to the practicalities of growing plants, you don't want to waste time and money with too many setbacks. So, first of all, find out how to choose the right plants, and then learn how to make them as happy and healthy as possible.

Choosing plants

A lot of work goes into making plants in a garden centre look deliciously tempting, and it's very easy to be beguiled into making impulse buys. But before you part with your hard-earned cash, spare a thought for the plant and find out whether it will be happy in the conditions you can offer it. An informed choice based on what you want the plant to do and how well it is likely to perform should result in a more satisfying purchase.

Good-value plants

Among the most worthwhile garden plants for cutting are the ones that offer a long season of usefulness. Some will be plants that flower sporadically over a long period, others will be 'multi-taskers' that offer two or more types of cutting material at different seasons, such as foliage and berries, coloured stems and catkins, or fragrant flowers and evergreen leaves. Of course there will also be short-lived, less hard-working plants that earn their place through sheer 'wow factor', but these become much more versatile if you have a range of alternative partners to inspire creative combinations. Whatever plants you choose though, be sure to have plenty of variety. You want a good balance of shrubs, perennials, bulbs and annuals or biennials.

The support squad

It's easy to fall for the stars of the show, but don't forget your flower arrangements need a supporting cast too. Having a good range of easy 'filler' plants conveniently to hand in the garden will inspire you with a world of creative possibilities.

Sprays of tiny flowers are useful: *Alchemilla mollis*, for example, is a real winner in sun or partial shade, its froth of lime green is a familiar and flattering partner for stronger flowers of many kinds. Fennel, gypsophila and white umbellifers such as *Ammi majus*, *Orlaya grandiflora* or even the short-lived common cow parsley (*Anthriscus sylvestris*) are useful in similar ways.

Foliage plants

Don't forget that leaves also have their part to play in arrangements. Small-leaved evergreen shrubs – perhaps a variegated box such as *Buxus sempervirens* 'Elegantissima', or *Osmanthus delavayi* – will be useful throughout the year. The dark, glossy leaves of *Sarcococca confusa* are larger but just as useful, and this indispensable little shrub has the double bonus of being very shade-tolerant and providing wafts of delicious fragrance, both in the

A striking mix of red-hot pokers and the good-value red valerian, which produces flowers sporadically from late spring through to autumn.

garden and in winter arrangements. Pale foliage makes a handsome foil for many other colours. *Elaeagnus* 'Quicksilver' adds an uplifting quality to both garden and vase, though it is deciduous so its lovely silvery leaves are a seasonal pleasure.

Euonymus fortunei 'Silver Queen' is very useful for all-year variegated greenery, adding a spring-like touch of green and white to many kinds of arrangement. In a tight space it can be grown as ground cover or on a north-facing wall or fence. For more on foliage, *see* page 59.

Plants for a long season of cut flowers

Anemone × *hybrida* 'Honorine Jobert'
Anthemis punctata subsp. *cupaniana*
Centranthus ruber
Cirsium rivulare 'Atropurpureum'
Cosmos bipinnatus
Cyclamen coum
Eryngium planum
Euphorbia cyparissias 'Fens Ruby'
Galanthus 'Atkinsii'
Helenium 'Sahin's Early Flowerer'

Right plant, right place

Your plants will always have a head start if you choose varieties that are compatible with the environment you can offer them. So do a little homework and if your garden is shady, or windy, or damp, go for plants that are naturally adapted to those conditions. Not only will they look more comfortable in their surroundings, they will also flourish better, need less attention, and produce more cutting material for the house.

Shady sites

Although shady areas of the garden have undoubted advantages, being able to grow masses of big, bright flowers for cutting isn't among them. Many annuals will struggle in shade, for example, and you may do better to concentrate on the subtler charms of interesting foliage and white flowers than to pin your hopes on riotously colourful perennials.

Many spring flowers, though, will be perfectly happy in gardens where the shade is provided by overhanging deciduous trees, whose opening leaves don't begin to cut out the light until most spring bulbs and perennials have flowered. Early bulbs likely to be successful include many snowdrops (*Galanthus*) and the whitish-blue *Scilla mischtschenkoana*, which flower well in shade and look wonderful among hellebores and pulmonaria, two of many spring perennials that flower well in gloomy spots. *Narcissus* 'Jack Snipe' is one of the more shade-tolerant varieties of daffodil. It shows up well in low light and its dainty shape and light effect make it an ideal cut flower. Grow it with ground-covering sweet woodruff (*Galium odoratum*), sweet cicely (*Myrrhis odorata*) or *Euphorbia amygdaloides* var. *robbiae* – shade-loving perennials that will lighten a dark corner and also expand at the right time to hide the fading leaves of spring bulbs.

Some (though not all) shrubs with variegated leaves will thrive in dark places: cultivars of *Euonymus fortunei* and the variegated box *Buxus sempervirens* 'Elegantissima' can both be relied on, even in low light, for pretty foliage that is perfect for cutting. Skimmias and sarcococcas are relatively compact, shade-tolerant shrubs that will contribute fragrant flowers to scent the house in early spring, as well as provide evergreen foliage.

Shelter and dappled shade suit an informal, woodland-style planting of hellebores and numerous bulbs, including starry, blue-flowered chionodoxas.

Suitable plants for challenging sites

SHADY SITES

Buxus sempervirens 'Elegantissima'

Cyclamen hederifolium

Euonymus fortunei 'Silver Queen'

Euphorbia amygdaloides var. *robbiae*

× *Fatshedera lizei*

Geranium 'Mavis Simpson'

Geranium phaeum 'Album'

Hedera

Helleborus

Hosta 'Wide Brim'

Polystichum setiferum

Pulmonaria 'Opal'

Sarcococca confusa

Skimmia × *confusa* 'Kew Green'

Vinca minor

Tellima grandiflora

WINDY SITES

Armeria maritima

Berberis

Centranthus ruber

Crocosmia

Cytisus × *praecox*

Dianthus

Elaeagnus angustifolia

Eryngium

Eucalyptus

Euphorbia

Hippophae rhamnoides

Nepeta

Pittosporum

A delightful planting scheme to shrug off coastal winds: sea kale, red valerian, broom, California poppies and *Leymus*.

A gravel mulch helps sustain a varied planting scheme of drought-tolerant grasses, heleniums and sea holly.

Windy sites

Trees, hedges and semi-permeable fencing make the best windbreaks, and providing some kind of shelter like this will make a big difference to what you can grow in an exposed garden. However, even when you have established some protection, trying to grow many of the classic cut flowers is likely to prove rather frustrating. You'll probably have to avoid anything that becomes top-heavy when in bloom, such as lupins, delphiniums, and double-flowered cultivars of dahlias or herbaceous peonies. Much more likely to succeed are plants with an airy structure, flexible or wiry stems,

and small leaves that are leathery or hairy. For foliage, try silvery sea buckthorn (*Hippophae rhamnoides*), purple berberis, *Elaeagnus angustifolia* or, in milder areas, pittosporums and eucalyptus.

Shrubs that originate in the Mediterranean, for example sage, rosemary and lavender, will provide both aromatic foliage and seasonal flowers, and brooms such as cultivars of *Cytisus × praecox* are also worth considering. If you can establish a variety of shrubs like these, they will provide year-round shelter for some tough herbaceous plants. Seaside wildflowers should be resilient in all but the coldest winds.

Dry soil

In summer, a dry garden may well struggle to produce colourful flowers for cutting, but usually there's enough rain in autumn and winter to start bulbs into growth, so these are often a good bet for dry gardens. For early spring, try some grape hyacinths (*Muscari*), scillas and chionodoxas – perfect for small arrangements. A little later, tulips and then alliums can be the stars of the cutting garden. All these will thrive better in well-prepared soil with plenty of humus to retain moisture, and perhaps a mulch of gravel or grit; as usual, the best way to cope with difficult growing

A collection of damp-loving plants in a late-summer border: the tall, dramatic red spikes of *Persicaria amplexicaulis* 'Firetail' provide a long-lasting season of colour and are good for cutting.

conditions is to improve the soil before planting (*see* opposite) and choose suitable plants.

Deep roots are another mechanism that enables plants to cope with dry gardens. The blooms of the deep-rooted oriental poppy (*Papaver orientale*), for example, may be short-lived when cut, but their unique combination of delicate petals, dramatic structure and flamboyant colour packs a punch that few other flowers achieve. If they are well conditioned (*see* page 40) and arranged in a suitable container, they can be a highlight of the year.

Mediterranean plants with evergreen aromatic leaves can be stalwarts of dry, sunny gardens. Sprigs of rosemary or bay are useful in arrangements all year, and if you have a sheltered corner, try growing a myrtle (*Myrtus communis*) for its lovely scented foliage – a traditional component of wedding bouquets.

Damp soil

Permanently waterlogged soil is bad news for many plants, but there are plenty more that are well adapted to damp conditions. A lot of them grow fast and make large plants – perfect if you have a taste for strong colours and space for big displays.

For a dramatic colour scheme, try partnering some of the bold red flowers of late summer, such as cultivars of damp-loving *Persicaria amplexicaulis* or *Lobelia cardinalis*, with the dark purple foliage of *Physocarpus opulifolius* 'Diabolo', which is also a good foil for the damp-loving types of euphorbia. These include the orange-red *Euphorbia griffithii* 'Fireglow' and the indispensable acid-green *Euphorbia palustris*.

Willows (*Salix*) have recently become fashionable in floristry. Provided you have plenty of damp ground in which to grow them

(away from buildings or drains), there are a number of shrubby types that are good value for both spring catkins and attractive foliage. They can be kept more manageable by cutting them hard back in winter. The hoary willow (*Salix elaeagnos* subsp. *angustifolia*) has wands of slender silvery leaves, while lovely red or violet winter stems are a feature of *Salix daphnoides* and the graceful *Salix purpurea* 'Nancy Saunders'. The nearest any catkins get to flamboyant – they're almost black, with red anthers – are those of *Salix gracilistyla* 'Melanostachys'.

Suitable plants for difficult soils

DRY SOIL	DAMP SOIL
Achillea	Aruncus dioicus
Briza maxima	Aster 'Little Carlow'
Centranthus ruber	Cornus alba 'Sibirica Variegata'
Cerinthe major 'Purpurascens'	Euphorbia palustris
Elaeagnus 'Quicksilver'	Euphorbia griffithii 'Fireglow'
Eryngium giganteum	Galanthus 'Magnet'
Euphorbia oblongata	Geum rivale 'Leonard's Variety'
Gypsophila paniculata	Leucojum vernum
Lavandula angustifolia	Lobelia cardinalis
Limonium platyphyllum	Persicaria amplexicaulis 'Firetail'
Nepeta 'Six Hills Giant'	Salix purpurea 'Nancy Saunders'
Nicandra physalodes	Zantedeschia aethiopica
Nigella damascena	

Preparing the soil

Gardeners are seldom blessed with ready-made perfect soil. When you're planning any kind of planting, effort invested in improving whatever type of soil you have will reap rewards every time. It's always so tempting to get seeds and plants in as soon as possible, but ultimately it's far more satisfying to create conditions that will get them off to a flying start, so they can really do you proud.

Goodbye weeds

The first task when you're making a new bed is to eradicate any perennial weeds. Bindweed, ground elder and couch grass tend to be among the most troublesome ones in flower borders, with nettles, docks and brambles almost as bad. All these can be tricky to get rid of, but if you're less than thorough they're certain to be back, and once the plants are in, weeds are much harder to control.

Turning the soil several times over a period of a few weeks is a good way to start. Autumn or early spring is the ideal time, whenever the soil isn't too wet and sticky. Remove every piece of root and shoot that you see. Annual weeds can be deeply buried as you dig.

Soil improvement

Once the soil is reasonably 'clean', dig the plot over again, this time incorporating some bulky compost or well-rotted manure. Humus-rich organic matter is second to none for putting life into your soil. The almost magical water-retaining properties of humus are invaluable in helping dry soils to retain moisture in a way that is constantly accessible to plant roots. Humus also encourages worms, which aerate the soil, especially beneficial on damp or compacted ground.

Now you can sit back, admire the results of your toil and plan your seed and plant purchases, while allowing the soil to settle. Just before you plant, turn the surface over again lightly, to get rid of any newly sprouted weeds. If you'll be sowing seeds, rake the surface until you have a neat, level seed bed with a surface of fine, crumbly soil.

Invest in your soil

Creating and maintaining a healthy soil is one of the first principles of good gardening. Your chief ally in this is a supply of bulky organic matter to put life into the soil. These days, coping with a load of farmyard or stable manure isn't practical for most of us, but it's easy and very satisfying to make your own garden compost. And if your local authority collects garden waste for recycling, they may also market the end product of their large-scale composting process – a valuable soil conditioner that is usually sold conveniently bagged, and is sometimes also available in loose loads for larger gardens.

Work generous amounts of well-rotted compost or other bulky organic material into the soil before planting.

Sowing and planting

There's nothing more magical than following a tiny seed on its journey towards a fully fledged flowering plant. Growing from seed is inexpensive and can be easy, but there can also be pitfalls along the way, so it's worth knowing a few basic tips to increase your chances of success. If it's instant impact you're after, you may prefer to buy young plants (*see* pages 36–7).

Plants for sowing

There are plenty of plants suitable for cutting that are easy to grow from seed.

Annuals

Most annuals grow quickly from seed and some can flower within a couple of months from sowing. They die after flowering, usually having set seed if they get the chance, providing next year's flowers with little or no effort on your part.

Hardy annuals are among the easiest plants to grow from seed. Many prefer to begin life outdoors in the place where they are to grow and flower. Most can be sown either in autumn or in spring. A notable exception for the cutting garden is sweet peas (*Lathyrus odoratus*), which are normally sown in pots indoors in autumn or early spring and then planted out.

Some annuals are half-hardy. These come from warmer climates and can't tolerate frost. They are sown in pots indoors in spring and are usually transplanted as small seedlings into trays or pots, where they have enough space to grow on

If you've never tried growing plants from seed, give it a go. It's one of the most rewarding gardening activities.

under cover and are planted out in late spring or early summer, when frosts are over.

Biennials

Biennials are plants that grow from seed their first year and then mature and flower the next.

Start off the seeds either in pots (better for very small seeds) or in outdoor drills, usually between mid-spring and early summer. Transplant the seedlings into rows in the garden to grow on until the autumn, when they can be moved to wherever you want them to flower the following year.

With biennials that set large quantities of seed, such as foxgloves (*Digitalis*), teasels (*Dipsacus*) and *Eryngium giganteum*, it is well worth scattering some fresh seed where you would like the plants to grow. There's nothing to lose, and the chances are some of the seed will take, saving the trouble and risk of moving seedlings.

Perennials

Although perennials are easier to grow from plants, it can be fun to raise new varieties from seed, and if you need a lot of one kind it will be less costly. Germination is often better with fresh seed, sown as soon as possible after collection. As with annuals and biennials, sowing in

pots will usually give the seedlings a better chance of success. Gardening friends and relatives may be a good source of fresh (and free) seed of cottage-garden perennials that seed generously, such as hellebores, verbascums, hollyhocks (*Alcea*), aquilegias and euphorbias.

Don't forget

Many half-hardy annuals can be bought in garden centres as bedding plants ready for planting out, but the range of varieties is limited in comparison with seed.

Suitable for sowing

ANNUALS	BIENNIALS
Antirrhinum	Dianthus barbatus
Briza maxima	Digitalis purpurea
Calendula officinalis	Dipsacus
Centaurea cyanus	Eryngium giganteum
Cerinthe major 'Purpurascens'	Erysimum
Consolida ajacis	Lunaria annua
Cosmos bipinnatus	Myosotis
Iberis umbellata	
Lathyrus odoratus	PERENNIALS
Moluccella laevis	Alcea
Nicandra physalodes	Alchemilla
Nigella damascena	Aquilegia
Papaver	Euphorbia
Tropaeolum majus	Geum
Zinnia	Helleborus
	Verbascum

Sowing under cover

Sowing seeds in pots indoors or in a greenhouse or cold frame rather than direct into the ground gives you much more control over the vulnerable early stages in the life of a plant. Seeds are likely to germinate more readily and get off to a good start if they are protected from garden hazards (inclement weather, slugs, cats, birds, weeds, and so on).

Small pots are best: they take up less space and are perfectly adequate for the initial seedling stage. Use a fresh, sterile seed compost for sowing, such as a John Innes mix. Most seed composts are moisture-retentive yet free-draining and low in nutrients, because too rich a compost can 'burn' the seedlings. As the seedlings' first 'true' leaves appear, they will need to be 'pricked out' to give individuals more space (*see* step 4, right).

Sowing outdoors

If you happen to strike lucky and choose the right moment, when the weather is favourable and pests are otherwise occupied, sowing seeds of hardy annuals outdoors where they

HOW TO sow seeds

Fill a small pot with fresh seed compost and gently firm and level the surface. Scatter the seeds evenly and thinly across the surface. Larger seeds can be individually placed. Avoid letting any of the seeds touch each other, since they will restrict each other's growth.

Sieve or sprinkle a thin layer of compost over the seeds. You can use vermiculite or perlite instead. Generally, small seeds need to be just covered, but larger ones should have a deeper layer over them. Stand the pots or trays in tepid water until the surface of the compost is damp.

Place the pots in a well-lit position, but not in full sun. Cover with a plastic bag to help with germination. Check the pots daily, watering sparingly if they are dry. Remove the bags when the seedlings appear.

'Prick out' each seedling by carefully teasing out each one (holding it by the leaves, not the stem) and transplanting them singly into compost-filled larger pots, for growing on to planting-out size.

are to flower can be the easiest thing in the world. Preparing the ground thoroughly (*see* page 33) will improve their chances of success. The soil needs to be forked and raked until it is fine and crumbly.

Don't forget

In dry weather, transplanted seedlings and any other new plantings that are not yet well established will be the first to suffer – so, when watering, be sure to make them a priority.

The seeds are best sown in straight rows so that you can more easily distinguish them from the weed seedlings that will inevitably come up with them. Space the rows quite generously, giving yourself room to access each row from at least one side for weeding and staking the young plants, and for gathering the flowers. Make shallow grooves, or 'drills', with a rake, hoe, trowel or bamboo cane and sow your seeds

Mark out each seed row using string tied to two canes and draw the corner of a hoe along the line to make a shallow groove, or 'drill'.

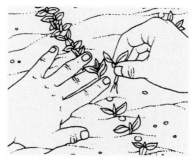

As soon as they are big enough to handle easily, thin out the seedlings to avoid overcrowding.

Don't forget

A surface mulch of compost or chipped bark, applied to damp soil at the end of a planting session, will help to suppress weeds and retain moisture in the soil, and will eventually break down to act as a soil conditioner.

Planting

Some plants are available as plug plants or pot-grown plants, which can be put straight into borders, creating instant impact.

Plug plants

An ever-increasing range of young plants can be bought in this form, available either individually or in packs by mail order and in garden centres and nurseries. Each plant is rooted into a 'plug' of compost. Plug plants are particularly well suited to fast-growing summer annuals. Unpack the plugs promptly and transfer them to larger pots to give them a few weeks' growing time before hardening them off (see opposite) and planting out.

into them quite sparingly. Seed packets often tell you how deep the seed should be; as a rule of thumb the larger the seed, the deeper the drill. Very small seeds should be only just covered. In dry weather, water the bottom of the drill before you sow, then when you cover the seeds with soil the moisture will be kept in.

Help prevent cats and birds disturbing your seed bed by covering it with netting or prickly twigs, and look out for slugs, which can quickly dispatch a row of tiny seedlings.

In favourable conditions, most hardy annuals will germinate within a week or two. Thin them while they're still small to give each room to develop properly, and keep the rows as weed-free as you can. Don't let them dry out, and water after thinning or weeding to settle the seedlings back into the soil.

Choose a mild, still day to put out bedding plants. Water them beforehand, give them adequate space to grow and water well after planting.

Shrubs and perennials

Shrubs and perennials for your cutting garden are most likely to be bought as pot-grown plants, which can be planted at almost any time of year when the weather is favourable. Damp, mild conditions are ideal, but avoid very windy weather or waterlogged soil. Ideally, plant after rain has soaked the plants in their pots. If the pots feel at all light or dry, soak them in a bucket of water for half an hour just before planting.

Give the plants a good start by preparing the soil well (*see* page 33). Let the soil settle before planting, and dig the holes just before you're ready to plant. In a new bed that has been well dug and thoroughly prepared, the hole need be only a little larger than the rootball of each plant; otherwise, it will need to be considerably larger. Turn the plant out of its pot, with a gentle tap if necessary, and try to keep the

rootball intact. Set the rootball in the hole, with the surface level with the soil surface. Firm the soil around it, and water to settle the roots.

Hardening off

Young plants that have been kept under cover, whether raised from seed or bought from a garden centre, must be acclimatized gradually to outdoor life before they're planted out permanently. Begin on a mild, still day by moving them to a sheltered place outdoors for a few hours. Steadily increase the time outside each day until you're just bringing them in at night. After a week or so they can be left out at night, if the weather is kind, until you're ready to plant them. Try to avoid windy weather for planting out, and be prepared to cover half-hardy plants with horticultural fleece at night if frost is forecast.

Spacing plants

There are so many variables in gardening, such as soil, site, plant habit and weather, that it's hard to give definitive advice on spacing your plants. But generally speaking, if cut flowers are your aim, it's better to have large, flourishing, well-spaced plants. The stems will be stronger, the blooms larger, and the flowering season of annuals and biennials won't be curtailed by the plant rushing to get its flowering over with, and seed set before it dies – as can happen with weak,

overcrowded or starved plants. Also, you'll want to space your plants so that you can access them easily for cutting. So be sure to thin plants grown from seed sown *in situ* (*see* pages 35–6) and be generous with the space when planting out.

Fast-growing plants, such as *Cosmos bipinnatus* and larger dahlias, mop up lots of nutrients and water and fill their space quickly; by the end of the season, a distance of 90cm (3ft) will look none too big. Large, heavy plants of this kind will need to be securely staked (*see* page 42). In raised beds and containers, with rich soil that is not compacted, plants can be packed in more closely, but take care not to let any delicate treasures become swamped by aggressive neighbours.

Plants grown under cover need to be acclimatized slowly to the outside world before being planted out.

Growing bulbs for cutting under cover

If you have a cold frame, greenhouse or conservatory you can grow a wider range of flowers to pick, especially for the colder months of the year. Another advantage is that the quality of the blooms will be better if they don't have to withstand the worst of the weather.

Bulbs are prime candidates for indoor cultivation. Some beautiful varieties are on the edge of hardiness, and with others flowering can be delayed by poor weather, especially in spring. So if you have a bit of space in the greenhouse border, try some of those that are easy to accommodate. *Anemone coronaria* corms can be planted in autumn and spring for a longer season of rich, intense colour. The frilly, delicate spring flowers of *Ranunculus asiaticus* really benefit from protection and must be kept dry when dormant in summer, so being under glass suits them. Freesias also benefit from growing under glass.

As a table centrepiece, an attractive bowl of choice, freshly cut edible leaves and flowers, carefully arranged, can be just as arresting as a floral display in a vase, while a handy bunch of garden herbs will enhance both the look of your kitchen and the taste of the dishes produced in it. You don't need a fully fledged vegetable garden to grow them: a well-prepared metre-square bed or even a collection of containers will suffice. Garden produce, grown and harvested with love and attention, can transform everyday eating into something much more special.

Growing your own herbs

Although many fresh herbs are readily available to buy these days, those that you can pick fresh from the garden are usually far superior in flavour and freshness. The cost of pre-packed herbs in supermarkets soon mounts up if you need several different kinds, and most herbs are easy to grow. Many are perennial, and some (such as mint and chives) will tolerate a fair amount of shade, while poor, dry soil is perfect for Mediterranean plants such as thymes and rosemary. With herbs that you grow yourself, you can harvest exactly as much or as little as you require without waste. Keep the plants close to the house so you can nip out from the kitchen and collect what you need. (For information on drying herbs, *see* box, page 41.)

Garden specialities

Certain herbs and salad leaves are difficult to find in the shops but make trouble-free garden plants. Sorrel, for instance, is practically indestructible once established, and is among the first plants to produce those long-awaited first edible leaves of the year, in early spring. Their shelf-life is short, but if you grow the leaves yourself you

This eye-catching salad contains a variety of leaves, including mizuna, mustard and lettuce, and edible nasturtium flowers.

can use them to create unusual seasonal sauces, omelettes and salads that seem to capture the very essence of spring. Lovage, similar to celery, is equally easy to grow and just as distinctive in flavour – but you seldom see its pungent leaves on sale. Sweet

Don't forget

A prettily tied bunch of garden-fresh herbs, a small basket of just-picked berries, or a decorative salad, can make a special gift to take along when visiting friends. Never underestimate the appeal to non-gardeners of the produce you take for granted!

Flowering vegetables

If you grow vegetables, it can be fun to leave a few in the ground at the end of the season and allow them to flower. In their second summer, carrots will produce beautiful filigree white flowers followed by intricate cage-like seedheads, while leeks turn into particularly architectural flowers, with handsome and long-lasting, teardrop-shaped buds that burst open into large violet-tinged globes in typical allium style. Chicory develops tall stems generously studded with dandelion-style flowers in a wonderful shade of blue. And parsnip flowers – statuesque, lacy and golden – have been seen in the gardens of several leading designers.

There are many easy-to-grow edible leaves that aren't readily available in the shops.
① Sweet cicely (*Myrrhis odorata*).
② Sorrel (*Rumex acetosa*).
③ Lovage (*Levisticum officinale*).
④ Chervil (*Anthriscus cerefolium*).

Some herb cultivars have particularly attractive foliage as well as tasting good.

① *Salvia officinalis* 'Tricolor' (tricoloured sage).

② *Thymus* 'Silver Posie' (silver lemon thyme).

③ *Foeniculum vulgare* 'Purpureum' (bronze fennel).

④ *Mentha suaveolens* 'Variegata' (variegated apple mint).

⑤ *Melissa officinalis* 'Aurea' (gold-variegated lemon balm).

⑥ *Petroselinum crispum* 'Moss Curled' (parsley).

cicely is a woodland plant that produces a mound of fresh, feathery foliage in early spring – invaluable in the garden for covering up the tatty leaves of fading spring bulbs, and useful in the kitchen for adding a spicy sweetness to fruit. Its daintier relative, chervil, is an annual grown from seed.

Ornamental herb cultivars

Armoracia rusticana 'Variegata' (variegated horseradish)

Chamaemelum nobile 'Flore Pleno' (chamomile)

Foeniculum vulgare 'Purpureum' (bronze fennel)

Melissa officinalis 'Aurea' (gold-variegated lemon balm)

Mentha suaveolens 'Variegata' (variegated apple mint)

Ocimum basilicum var. *purpurascens* 'Purple Ruffles' (purple basil)

Origanum vulgare 'Country Cream' (variegated pot marjoram)

Petroselinum crispum 'Moss Curled' (parsley)

Rosmarinus officinalis 'Severn Sea' (rosemary)

Salvia officinalis 'Purpurascens' (purple sage)

Salvia officinalis 'Tricolor' (tricoloured sage)

Thymus 'Silver Posie' (silver lemon thyme)

It is a classic ingredient of the French cook's *fines herbes*, and is another spring herb that is seldom in shops but easy to grow. The feathery leaves and unique flavour are an asset to both garden and kitchen, and if you leave it to set seed it will often self-sow.

Decorative herbs

Some herb plants earn their space by being pretty enough for a vase as well as useful for the kitchen. Cultivars with especially ornamental leaves include variegated types of lemon balm, thyme, sage or pot marjoram, bronze fennel and ornamental mints (*see* box, left, and above). As well as giving a long season of foliage interest in the garden, they make useful material for posies for the house, and most of them smell wonderful, both indoors and out.

Edible flowers

Edible flowers aren't only for chic restaurants. They feature in traditional recipes for crystallized violets, lavender shortbread and elderflower cordial.

The dainty, true-blue flowers of borage are familiar today in summer drinks, while deep-fried courgette flowers are a speciality of the Italian kitchen.

Contemporary cooks use other vegetable and herb flowers, such as those of peas and broad beans, which can be used in salads and other dishes or as a garnish. Brightly coloured red, yellow or orange nasturtiums can bring a touch of drama to a green salad, and many other edible flowers to try include pot marigolds (*Calendula officinalis*), primroses, honeysuckle, violets and cowslips.

Pot marigold (*Calendula officinalis*) and borage: both edible flowers.

Cutting and preparing plant material

If you can gather your own flowers and foliage straight from the garden, they should not need complicated conditioning to give them a longer life. Their freshness will give them a head start, and they need not be long out of water. But a few simple measures will improve the flowers' ability to take up water once cut, helping them to stay fresh and making it more worthwhile taking trouble over arranging them.

Cutting stems

Early morning or evening are the best times to gather flowers from the garden. Cut the stems with sharp, clean scissors or secateurs (or a knife) and put them into water as soon as possible after cutting – best of all, take a bucket or jug of water out into the garden with you. The water should not be straight from the cold tap: stems absorb tepid water more easily.

For best results, recut the stems at an angle (some say while they are still under water) and leave the flowers in the bucket or jug in a cool place overnight before arranging them. Remove the leaves from the lower part of the stem so that no leaves are under the water. Slit woody stems at the base and/or remove some of the bark up to about 5cm (2in) from the bottom of the stem. (Some people prefer to hammer the base of the stems.)

Plunge freshly picked flowers and foliage straight into a bucket of tepid water and leave them in a cool place.

Conditioning tips

Searing the stems of poppies, euphorbias, hellebores and other flowers that are prone to flopping can help to prolong their vase life. Cut off the base of the stems and dip the bottom 2.5–5cm (1–2in) into a jug of boiling water for up to a minute. This technique works with woody-stemmed plants, too, and can also rescue cut flowers that have already flopped.

Florists have a range of other specialist tactics that are useful for particular flowers. For example, a bunch of tulips can be conditioned to keep them straight-stemmed by binding the stems together quite tightly all the way up, with twine or newspaper, and standing the bunch in water. Leave the flowers to stand for a few hours like this before untying and arranging them. Piercing each stem crossways with a needle, just below the flower, will also help the tulips to stay upright.

A few hours before arranging tulips, bind the stems together and stand the bunch in water. Pierce each stem with a needle, just below the flower.

Special additives are helpful in conditioning the water for cut flowers, helping to prevent bacteria build-up as well as feeding the flowers. You can either buy commercial flower food (follow the manufacturer's instructions) or make your own: add to each 1 litre (2 pints) of water half a teaspoon of household bleach and a teaspoon each of sugar and lemon juice or vinegar.

Always wash vases thoroughly with hot, soapy water, using a bottle brush if necessary. Awkward corners where grime has built up can sometimes be cleaned by adding a spoonful of grit to the washing water and swirling it around.

Don't forget

Flowers that are members of the cabbage family, for instance wallflowers, stocks, honesty and candytuft, need frequent changes of water to keep them fresh and sweet-smelling.

Dried flowers and foliage

A well-planned cutting garden will give you something to pick pretty well throughout the year, but there may still be odd gaps, especially from early to midwinter, when dried flowers and seedheads may be a welcome alternative. They can also be useful as Christmas decorations (*see* page 63). Drying flowers is a craft in itself, sometimes involving complicated procedures and potions to preserve textures and colours, but there are many attractive plants that are very straightforward to dry.

Pick plants in their prime

It can be very tempting to try to have the best of both worlds by first enjoying a plant in flower in the garden and then cutting it for drying. Occasionally this can work, but many flowers, if picked when past their best, will drop their petals during the drying process or soon afterwards. Gathering the stems just before the flowers are fully open usually gives the best results. Choose a dry day, and take off the lower leaves from each stem as you go.

The drying process

Most flowers and seedheads are best hung upside down to dry. This helps the stems to stiffen so they stay upright. Tie them in bundles with the flowerheads or seedheads staggered so they don't interlock. Choose a warm, dry, airy place: a porch may be suitable, or in damp weather an airing cupboard or shed, or above a radiator. Suspend the bunches from hooks, or use clips or pegs to fix them to coathangers or a length of twine, clothes-line style, and leave them until they're totally crisp and dry. This will probably take up to a couple of weeks.

Some plants will look more natural when dried if you stand them upright

Hang flowers upside down in a warm, dry place and leave them for a week or two until they are completely dry.

or lay them flat during the drying process. This applies to stems with dangling flowerheads or seedpods, such as honesty, the quaking grass *Briza maxima* and love-lies-bleeding (*Amaranthus caudatus*), and to hydrangeas and achilleas.

Easy plants for drying

Acanthus	Limonium sinuatum
Achillea	Lunaria annua
Allium cristophii	seedheads
Amaranthus	Nicandra physalodes
caudatus	seedheads
Briza maxima	Nigella damascena
Dipsacus fullonum	Papaver somniferum
Echinops	seedheads
Eryngium	Physalis alkekengi
Hydrangea	seedheads
Iris foetidissima	Salvia viridis
seedheads	Xerochrysum
	bracteatum

Opium poppies have decorative pepper-pot seedheads that look great when they're dried. Cut them before they turn brown on the plant.

Dried herbs for the kitchen

Some culinary herbs, notably sage, rosemary and bay, can be picked fresh from the garden all year round. Others, including parsley, chives, tarragon and chervil, lose their character when dried and anyway can be bought fresh for much of the year. A third group, mostly sun-loving culinary herbs such as basil and sweet marjoram, produce an abundance of pungent aromatic foliage in summer but dislike winter cold. They are better used fresh, of course, but it is worth drying any surplus, while the leaves are young, flavoursome and fresh, as a winter alternative to use in cooking. Gather leafy stems on a sunny day and dry them gently on trays in a very low oven or airing cupboard. Store the leaves when completely dry, whole if possible, in airtight jars to use in winter.

Maintaining your cutting garden

Cut flowers and foliage are in a sense a crop, and achieving good yields from your cutting garden will be just as important as keeping the beds and borders looking attractive. Help your plants to perform well by giving them the ongoing attention they need at each stage of their life cycle.

Feeding and watering

The need to spend time on feeding and watering can be significantly reduced by choosing the right plants for your garden (*see* pages 30–2) and preparing the soil really well before planting (*see* page 33).

Once your cutting garden is established, just keep the soil in good heart with an annual spring boost in the form of a mulch of well-rotted manure or garden compost, applied while the soil is damp. Hungry plants such as roses, dahlias and delphiniums may benefit from an extra feed of general fertilizer, but avoid overfeeding plants because they will simply be encouraged to make too much lush growth. Watering should be required only in prolonged dry weather or for new plantings.

Overhauling a mixed border

If you're growing your flowers and foliage for cutting in a mixed border that is densely packed with shrubs, perennials, bulbs and annuals, it can be hard to know when to carry out basic maintenance. Going through the bed thoroughly once a year, pruning any shrubs and dividing perennials as necessary, will prevent overcrowding and ensure that the more vigorous plants don't take over, while also rejuvenating clumps that have exhausted their soil and begun to die out in the middle. The best time to do this is in early spring. Weeds can be removed before they become a serious problem, and most bulbs will be visible above ground, so you won't damage them unwittingly.

Weeding

Your plants will thrive much better without competition from annual or perennial weeds, and you'll avoid the dispiriting feeling of letting things get out of control if you keep on top of them. Weeding regularly, just a few minutes at a time, can be a pleasurable occupation and keeps you in touch with your plants, but there's no need to panic if you've missed a few days. The two most important things are to dig out any perennial weeds such as bindweed and ground elder before they become a problem, and to remove annual weeds before they set seed.

Supporting your plants

You'll need to make sure flowers for cutting have the necessary support to prevent them flopping over – which can result in bent stems or, worse still, mud stains, broken stems and slug damage.

Annuals, particularly, grow fast and can quickly become top-heavy, while certain perennials, such as medium to tall campanulas and asters, oriental poppies (*Papaver orientale*) and alstroemerias, will look more attractive in the garden, and be in better condition for picking, if you've given them some form of support. Use twiggy stems to hold the flowers in place, or canes and string threaded, cat's-cradle style, among the stems. This is especially

Tie plants regularly to their supports. It will prevent stems flopping, and you can enjoy the flowers close up.

important in wet or windy weather, but to be on the safe side it's worth installing supports before the plants need it – much easier than trying to rescue the situation once they have fallen over.

Some tall plant spikes, for example delphiniums, will need staking individually, and of course climbers such as sweet peas and climbing nasturtiums need a structure such as a trellis or fence, or a wigwam of canes and twine, to scramble up.

Pruning

Flowering shrubs and climbers need to be kept vigorous if they are to continue to produce large, healthy blooms. Those that flower on new shoots, such as buddleias, *Hydrangea paniculata*, caryopteris and late-flowering clematis, are usually cut hard back at the start of the growing season to stimulate them into producing new stems on which they will flower after midsummer. Shrubs such as philadelphus and lilac, which blossom in late spring and early summer, carry their flowers on older wood, but still need to be constantly rejuvenated by the removal of tired old stems to make room for new shoots. Immediately after flowering, cut out some of the oldest branches right down to the base.

The colourful winter stems of dogwoods, such as cultivars of *Cornus alba* and *Cornus sanguinea*, tend to fade as the branches age, so ensure a good display of young, brighter wood by removing some of the oldest stems each year in spring.

Dead-heading

Removing dead flowerheads makes any garden look better, but it's especially vital if you're growing flowers for cutting. You'll want as many flowers as possible from each plant, and if plants are prevented from setting seed, many of them (especially sweet peas and a lot of other annuals, but also some perennials) will continue flowering.

Regular dead-heading keeps displays looking good and helps to encourage continued flowering.

Perennials that should be a priority when you're dead-heading include penstemons, heleniums, catmint (*Nepeta*), anthemis, *Campanula persicifolia*, *Salvia × superba* and *Lychnis coronaria*. Don't forget the repeat-flowering roses, as they will bloom again later. Try not to leave unsightly stalks, but cut off the spent flower complete with its supporting stem, all the way back to the next bud or shoot. Remember to leave a few seedheads of the plants you would like to self-sow, including foxgloves and annual poppies.

Dividing perennials

Just as shrubs can be kept vigorous by pruning, so many perennials can be rejuvenated if you divide clumps that have grown old and become less prolific. Some, such as achilleas, phlox and Michaelmas daisies, benefit from this treatment every year or two, while others may go on for many years without needing it.

If you've decided to rejuvenate a plant in this way, dig up the whole thing in early spring and break or chop off some younger, vigorous pieces from the outside edge of the clump – often, these will look like separate little rooted plants. Fork over the planting area, adding some compost or manure, and replant the pieces in the refreshed soil.

Cutting down

Some perennials should be cut down to the ground after flowering, either because their season is over and they won't flower again until next year, or to prevent excessive seeding, or because they will grow a fresh crop of leaves to replace their dead flowers and tired foliage. Those that should be cut include *Alchemilla mollis*, *Aquilegia*, *Centaurea montana*, *Centranthus ruber*, *Lychnis chalcedonica*, *Papaver orientale* and many of the earlier-flowering hardy geraniums such as *Geranium × magnificum*.

Don't forget

Be careful not to accidentally dead-head plants whose faded flowers turn into attractive seedheads that you'll be able to cut for indoors later in the year. These include sedums, acanthus, cardoons, eryngiums, pulsatillas, *Nigella damascena* and *Phlomis russeliana*.

Dividing clumps of perennials keeps them growing and flowering well. It also gives you new plants for free!

Plant problems and remedies

Pests and diseases have been around as long as gardening, but these days we are all encouraged to take a more relaxed attitude to them rather than reaching immediately for the sprayer. Growing your plants well is the first line of defence. Healthy plants shrug off problems more easily. Cultivate a good mix of plants, and if you find a particular plant seems pest-prone, just remember there are plenty of cutting plants available and it's easy to switch to something else instead. Lastly, encourage natural predators. Ladybirds, hoverflies, spiders, birds and even wasps can despatch large numbers of nuisance insects and their larvae without any effort on your part.

Common pests

Aphids

Greenfly are the most common form of these tiny sap-sucking insects, which can build up large populations very quickly, especially in hot, dry weather. Signs of aphids include distorted and/or sticky leaves. They also spread viruses and other plant diseases.

Prevention and control Try to spot their presence as soon as possible before one or two have become hundreds or thousands. Wipe them off stems and leaves (don't forget the underside) with a tissue or small paintbrush dipped in soapy water, or with your fingers, and examine affected plants regularly to make sure you have got them all. Aphids should become less of a problem as summer advances and populations of their predators, such as ladybirds and hoverflies, increase. Avoid spraying if possible, as sprays will kill these predators too. Certain flowers, for example eryngiums, poppies and verbascums, are attractive to hoverflies, so try to include such plants in your cutting garden.

Caterpillars

A healthy butterfly and moth population indicates a good garden ecosystem, but what to do about the plant-eating larvae of some species remains a conundrum for gardeners.

Prevention and control With the notable exception of the whites, whose caterpillars devour cabbages and their relatives, we tend to welcome butterflies, though moths perhaps not quite as much. Where caterpillars cause extensive plant damage it tends to be localized, so they are easy to see and pick off. Birds and wasps are valuable caterpillar predators, too. Plants to watch include verbascums, which can be devoured by caterpillars of the mullein moth, and euonymus and sedums, which are increasingly targeted by ermine moths whose caterpillars live in conspicuous silken 'tents' like dense cobwebs, where birds can't reach them. Defoliated roses may reveal the presence of small sawfly caterpillars; pick them off quickly before they pupate and become egg-laying adults.

Lily beetle

Conspicuous red beetles on lilies or fritillaries are bad news. Both adults and their unlovely larvae, which cover themselves in brown slime that looks like bird droppings, devour foliage and ruin plants.

Prevention and control Keep an eye open for any damage to lily leaves, and inspect plants regularly on sunny days, when the beetles are most likely to be active. The adults are easy to spot but harder to catch, so nab them quickly, and destroy any larvae that you see too.

Slugs and snails

Seedlings, young transplants and plants that are struggling are most likely to be targeted by these unwelcome pests, which are always worse in damp gardens and in mild, rainy weather.

Prevention and control Catching slugs and snails 'red-handed' and picking them off is the best remedy. You know you have caught them and prevented them breeding. Also, no slug or snail predators, such as thrushes and hedgehogs, have been put at risk by eating slugs that have absorbed toxins from pellets. Search for them with a torch on mild, damp evenings, looking not only among your plants but also under any pots and debris where they may lurk. A pot of salt solution will kill them fairly quickly.

Vine weevils

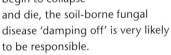

Adult vine weevils content themselves with nibbling leaves, but their grubs can quickly destroy plants by eating their roots. Plants in containers are especially vulnerable.

Prevention and control If a plant suddenly wilts, check around the roots for the plump white larvae and destroy them. Nursery compost is now often specially treated to protect plants from attack, and a biological control is available for use in the garden.

Common diseases

Damping off

When young seedlings germinate and, often a few days later, suddenly begin to collapse and die, the soil-borne fungal disease 'damping off' is very likely to be responsible.

Prevention and control Use fresh, good-quality compost, sow thinly, and 'prick out' seedlings to give each one more space, air and light as soon as they have their first 'true' leaves. Do not overwater newly emerged seedlings; most prefer to be only just damp. Ventilate frames and greenhouses well; fungal diseases spread in stagnant air.

Honey fungus

This disease can be fatal to both woody and herbaceous plants. Suspect it if a tree or shrub dies inexplicably, especially if the soil around it contains black threads like bootlaces, or if you notice a mushroomy smell or honey-brown toadstools.

Prevention and control Those who garden where honey fungus lurks have no option but to resign themselves to losing plants sometimes. There are no good chemical controls, and the best you can do is to avoid planting particularly susceptible species, such as birches and lilacs. Research has suggested that some species (including bay, box and yew) may have some resistance. Underground barriers of heavy-gauge polythene may help prevent the fungus from spreading to healthy plants that you are anxious to keep.

Powdery mildew

Plants that have become dry at the roots are more likely to be affected by powdery mildew, a fungal disease that causes an unsightly, dirty-white coating on leaves. The foliage turns yellow and distorted and growth is stunted.

Prevention and control Mulching the soil to keep it damp can be quite helpful, and it is possible to buy mildew-resistant forms of certain particularly susceptible plants such as Michaelmas daisies and bergamot. In the case of aquilegias, pulmonarias and other plants whose foliage tends to get mildew after a spring flowering, you can cut the plant down to the ground and it will grow a new set of mildew-free leaves.

Rust

Hollyhocks, snapdragons, roses and some alliums are among the plants likely to develop rusts – fungal diseases that often manifest themselves in small, brownish spots beneath the leaves of affected plants.

Prevention and control Improve air circulation; pick off badly affected leaves if possible, and renew plants regularly from seed or fresh bulbs where appropriate. Resistant varieties are often available, and worth seeking out.

Viruses

Virus diseases are to blame for a lot of incurable plant problems, many of them host-specific. If there is no other obvious reason for a plant developing blotchy, distorted or yellowing leaves, then a virus may well be responsible.

Prevention and control Many plant viruses are spread by aphids and other sap-sucking pests as they travel from plant to plant, so controlling such insects effectively is sure to help prevent disease. Once a plant is affected by a virus, there's nothing you can do but destroy the plant to prevent the disease from spreading.

Season by season

One of the best things about having home-grown flowers and foliage in the house is that they help you to capture and savour the best of each season. From the opening of the first snowdrop to the gathering of the last holly berries for Christmas, a garden that has been thoughtfully planned for year-round cutting will give you something different to pick, and many other things to look forward to, in every single week of the year.

Plants for year-round interest

A good plan for an all-year cutting garden is to combine a few special flowers for each month with a core of reliable, hard-working stalwarts that have a long period of interest. These should either flower for a long time (or repeatedly) over one season or provide you with different kinds of cutting material at different times of the year. You'll also need a few plants chosen as complementary foliage back-up for a range of flowers. With these three groups, you'll never be stuck for something to pick.

The evergreen shrub *Luma apiculata* 'Glanleam Gold' provides dainty variegated foliage all year round.

Hard-working flowers

Reliable, long-flowering plants are ideal for cutting. On their own, they may eventually seem monotonous, but if combined with other, different flowers in succession throughout the season, you won't ever tire of them. Catmint (*Nepeta*) and red valerian (*Centranthus ruber*), for example, flower for much of the summer with alliums, irises, geraniums and roses. If you cut them back, they will put on a second show in the autumn with asters, echinaceas and sedums. Among those plants that have more than one season of interest, sedums are especially useful, with buds, flowers and seedheads providing cutting material from late summer to winter. Euphorbias, anthemis and Japanese anemones (*Anemone × hybrida* and *Anemone hupehensis* var. *japonica*) also earn their keep well.

Evergreen foliage

No matter how small your garden, be sure to plant a few carefully chosen evergreens for a variety of foliage to partner your cut flowers. Compact shrubs, such as small-leaved hebes, fragrant rosemary and lavender, or the variegated *Luma apiculata* 'Glanleam Gold', will provide sprigs for many a petite display, while the foliage of numerous larger shrubs, for example pittosporums and osmanthus, makes an impact in the garden all year as well as providing cutting material. Evergreens that tolerate hard cutting back, including yew, box and hollies, are very versatile and easy to keep to size. The florist's favourite, *Eucalyptus gunnii*, is a vigorous plant but can be pruned hard every year to keep you supplied with its elegant, silvery-blue juvenile foliage that complements flowers of so many kinds.

More evergreens for year-round foliage

Atriplex halimus	*Hedera helix* cultivars
Aucuba japonica 'Crotonifolia'	*Lonicera nitida* 'Baggesen's Gold'
Azara microphylla 'Variegata'	*Myrtus communis*
Berberis darwinii	*Ophiopogon planiscapus* 'Nigrescens'
Brachyglottis Dunedin Group 'Sunshine'	*Prunus lusitanica*
Danae racemosa	*Rhamnus alaternus* 'Argenteovariegata'
Euonymus fortunei	*Rosmarinus officinalis*
Fatsia japonica	
Hebe rakaiensis	

If they are kept regularly dead-headed, late-summer flowers such as dahlias, zinnias, rudbeckias and *Ammi visnaga* should last until the first frosts.

Spring

Organizing flowers for the house through the winter often entails making a little go a long way, so it's a real treat when spring bulbs and blossom are out there in quantities that allow you to cut them generously. Bulbs play a starring role, but spring just wouldn't be spring without buds and catkins, the flowers of early perennials, and fresh new foliage too.

Spring bulbs

The flowers of most bulbs are well suited to cutting, so buy plenty of extra bulbs each year. If this seems wickedly extravagant when you're ordering, just remind yourself how inexpensive most bulbs are in comparison with bought cut flowers. By the time spring comes and the bulbs are flowering, you'll be glad you didn't economize. Either plant them in rows in a cutting patch, vegetable garden or allotment, or increase the numbers in grass and in borders so that you can cut what you need without denuding the garden. Don't worry, cutting the flowers will not harm the bulb, but be patient and always let the foliage die down naturally so that all the goodness from the leaves can return to the bulb and prepare it for flowering again next year.

If you're ordering bulbs from a specialist company that supplies unusual varieties as well as the more popular ones, choose a few each year that you haven't grown before. The widow iris (*Iris tuberosa*), with its almost sinister green-and-black

Bring some apple blossom indoors to enjoy its subtle fragrance and beauty as the pink buds open.

flowers, is an uncommon one for a dry, sunny spot. It flowers very early, and is lovely to pick so that its subtle colours and faint fragrance can be appreciated up close.

Grape hyacinths (*Muscari*), scillas and chionodoxas of various kinds are very easy to grow and can be fitted into even the smallest garden in generous numbers, providing a haze

Don't forget

Dead-head as many spring bulbs as you can when their flowers start to fade. Removing the seedheads prevents the plant from channelling energy into setting seed, allowing it to build up reserves for next year's flowers.

Unusual spring bulbs for cutting

Camassia quamash
Chionodoxa luciliae 'Alba'
Iris tuberosa
Muscari aucheri 'Ocean Magic'
Narcissus 'Waterperry'
Scilla bifolia
Tulipa montana
Tulipa 'Peppermintstick'

Allium hollandicum coincides with late tulips, giving scope for many different colour mixes. Let the alliums self-sow to create a massed planting like this.

of early colour in the garden as well as plenty of flowers for petite arrangements. Try the pink and white varieties, such as *Chionodoxa* 'Pink Giant' and *Scilla siberica* 'Alba', as well as the familiar blue.

Planting partners

A generous bunch of tulips, narcissi or other spring bulbs works well alone in a jug, but if you don't have many of a particular kind it's handy to be able to arrange flowering bulbs with other flowers and foliage.

Ivies, evergreen euonymus or the dark, elegantly divided leaves of *Helleborus foetidus* make excellent companions for early-spring bulbs, as do the prettily marbled green-and-white leaves of *Arum italicum* subsp. *italicum* 'Marmoratum' – a classic partner for snowdrops. A bit

Spring brings a variety of yellow and blue flowers to the garden. Primroses (*Primula*) and periwinkle (*Vinca*) go together just as well in a vase.

Narcissus 'Ice Wings', seen here with a mixture of grape hyacinth (*Muscari*) cultivars, is one of several useful white narcissi that go with everything.

Don't forget

Try to choose a damp day to dig up and divide clumps of snowdrops in late spring, as the foliage dies down. Split each clump into individual bulbs and replant them, to the same depth, in small groups where you would like to establish new colonies.

Plants for spring fragrance

Choisya × *dewitteana* 'Aztec Pearl'
Convallaria majalis
Daphne tangutica
Dianthus barbatus
Elaeagnus 'Quicksilver'
Erysimum cheiri
Hesperis matronalis var. *albiflora* 'Alba Plena'
Hyacinthus orientalis
Narcissus poeticus var. *recurvus*
Osmanthus × *burkwoodii*
Skimmia × *confusa* 'Kew Green'
Syringa
Viola odorata

---

later, the tiny white flowers of sweet woodruff (*Galium odoratum*) are a lovely fresh-looking vase companion for dwarf narcissi and small tulips, or for primulas. Late-spring partners include the wiry, pale green and then pinkish spires of *Tellima grandiflora* and the airy bronze flowerheads of the variegated woodrush *Luzula sylvatica* 'Marginata' – both are understated, pretty, and trouble-free as ground-cover plants for a shady spot.

Although herbaceous colour doesn't really get into its stride until early summer, there are a number of earlier-flowering border perennials that make colourful companions for bulbs. Pulmonarias and brunneras are among the early arrivals in shady spots, yielding attractive foliage as well as flowers for arrangements. *Ajuga reptans*, euphorbias, and the useful bright yellow daisy *Doronicum orientale* follow on in more open areas. The colours of all these make them an excellent fit

with the mainly blue, yellow and white palette of spring. As more perennials appear on the scene, there will be a reliable supply of cottage-garden flowers for cutting: these might include aquilegias, catmint (*Nepeta*), *Centaurea montana*, *Geum rivale* and Welsh poppies (*Meconopsis cambrica*). These easy-to-grow, resilient plants

Don't overlook foliage. The varied leaves of heucheras and pulmonarias stay attractive and provide cutting material for many months.

Rhododendron 'Jolie Madame' is one of many deciduous azaleas that can be cut to bring a touch of pure exotic colour to spring vases.

Exochorda × macrantha 'The Bride' is not only a lovely wedding flower but a good planting partner too – here, for *Clematis* 'Helsingborg'.

conveniently carry on flowering after the main flush of spring bulbs, bridging the gap before early-summer colour takes centre stage.

The blossom of early-flowering shrubs is fleeting, but it's still worth picking sprigs of spiraea, viburnum or exochorda for their pretty, white flowers, or rhododendrons and azaleas for their flamboyant ones. Also, many spring shrubs are wonderfully fragrant (*see* page 49).

Gold-laced primulas make delightful table decorations. This one combines beautifully with the golden pollen of goat willow (*Salix caprea*).

Spring trees

Swelling buds and catkins are among the first signs that a new season is just beginning to stir the plant world into activity. Bring a few hazel (*Corylus avellana*) twigs into the house as the catkins begin to expand, and watch for the tiny, bright red female flowers that nobody seems to notice; these eventually become hazelnuts. Stems can also be cut in early spring from various willows (*Salix*) as their furry, silky buds begin to swell and open. If these are kept dry rather than put in water, their development is arrested and they will stay as 'pussy willow' for many weeks.

A little later, the brand-new foliage of deciduous trees brings special pleasure after all the evergreens of winter. The moment passes so quickly that it's a pity not to bring some twigs into the house to watch in close-up as the leaves magically expand. Horse chestnut (*Aesculus hippocastanum*) is among the earliest to make its dramatic appearance, its

fat, sticky buds metamorphosing into bright green palmate leaves. In mid- to late spring, collect a few twigs of oak and beech as their buds begin to unfurl. The young leaves should last for a few days in a room that is not too warm, especially if the stems are conditioned first (*see* page 40). They can work well in arrangements, but a few stems displayed alone in a slender vase also make a simple but striking feature that you won't see again for another whole year.

Capture the moment

Many spring flowers are short-lived, but that's no reason not to enjoy them in the house – in fact, it makes them seem even more special. A few small twigs of apple blossom, or a stem of winter-flowering honeysuckle, for instance *Lonicera fragrantissima*, in a small vase on a desk or bedside table, will bring the feeling of spring indoors. Sprigs of pure white plum blossom or *Spiraea thunbergii* in early-spring arrangements have the same sparkling-fresh effect, partnered with daffodils and euphorbia. The petals will soon fall, but most probably replacement stems will still be conveniently to hand just outside the door.

Whatever the weather ...

Cool, wet spring days may be unwelcome if you want to be out there gardening, but they're a great ally for spring flowers, helping them to last longer in both garden and house. Make the most of any chilly spells to cut and enjoy spring blossom and other flowers that you wouldn't normally try indoors.

Don't forget

In late spring or early summer, look out for seedlings growing in inconvenient places. Foxgloves, honesty, aquilegias, eryngiums, violets, red valerian and sweet rocket are well worth transplanting while small (ideally in showery weather) to a better spot.

Wildflowers for cutting

Who can resist a bunch of freshly picked wildflowers? Primroses, sweet violets, poppies or ox-eye daisies have more simple, natural charm than any bouquet money can buy. Flowers like these are very easy to grow provided you choose the right kinds for your soil and conditions.

Gardening for wildlife

Gardens have become increasingly important as refuges for wildflowers and the insects they support, including hoverflies, butterflies, moths and bees. Wildlife gardening entails growing a wide mixture of plants that have something to offer your fellow garden residents. In the case of flowers, this usually means nectar for the butterflies and bees, and seeds to keep birds going in the winter. There are many plants that will fit the bill. Try to include at least a few native species – some make excellent cut flowers.

Garden wildflowers for cutting

Corn cockle (*Agrostemma githago*)
Cuckoo flower (*Cardamine pratensis*)
Pendulous sedge (*Carex pendula*)
Greater knapweed (*Centaurea scabiosa*)
Foxglove (*Digitalis purpurea*)
Teasel (*Dipsacus fullonum*)
Snakeshead fritillary (*Fritillaria meleagris*)
Sweet woodruff (*Galium odoratum*)
Field scabious (*Knautia arvensis*)
Ox-eye daisy (*Leucanthemum vulgare*)
Woodrush (*Luzula sylvatica*)
Cowslip (*Primula veris*)
Primrose (*Primula vulgaris*)
Pasque flower (*Pulsatilla vulgaris*)
Common valerian (*Valeriana officinalis*)
Sweet violet (*Viola odorata*)

Woodland flowers

A garden with shrubs and trees is quite similar to a deciduous woodland habitat, which favours plants that flower early in the year before the overhead leaf canopy creates too much shade. Examples of these are primroses and violets, bluebells, wood spurge, sweet woodruff and Solomon's seal. Add to these foxgloves, cow parsley, red campion, bugle and other plants of the woodland edge, which need a little more sunshine, and you have a good mixture of wildflowers for cutting. Typically they do not last long when cut, but they are so pretty that it's a pity not to enjoy some of them indoors, if only for a few days.

Making poppies last

With their fragile papery petals and arresting colour, field poppies (*Papaver rhoeas*) are among the brightest and prettiest wildflowers to have indoors, but they soon look a sorry sight if they are not conditioned properly. The stems of all poppies have a milky sap that quickly dries on contact with the air, preventing them from taking up water. Pick poppies as soon as they have opened, before bees pollinate them, and dip the freshly cut stem ends in boiling water (*see* page 40). Give the flowers a deep drink in tepid water for several hours or overnight. Treat all poppies – annual, biennial, perennial – like this, and you'll be able to enjoy them in close-up for a few days.

Create your own tiny spring woodland area with some wildflowers.
① English bluebells (*Hyacinthoides non-scripta*).
② Sweet violets (*Viola odorata*).

Grassland flowers

Either sow an annual wildflower mixture in a spare area of cultivated ground, or create a mini-meadow by leaving one area of grass uncut. Yarrow and speedwells may well appear by themselves, and you can add cowslips, ox-eye daisies, knapweeds and others. The annual wildflower yellow rattle (*Rhinanthus minor*) is worth including because it is semi-parasitic on grass, so helps to prevent it from swamping the flowers. The best way to establish wildflowers in grass is to buy 'plugs' – small plants rooted into a plug of compost. Plant them in damp weather, ideally in early autumn, to help the plants establish well.

All kinds of summer wildflowers bring great charm to simple flower arrangements.
① Field poppy (*Papaver rhoeas*).
② Ragged robin (*Lychnis flos-cuculi*).

Summer

Very gradually in some years, but in others quite suddenly, the freshness of spring evolves into the abundance of summer. Gardens are at their most generous, and you might be thinking there's no need to cut flowers to bring indoors as well. But it's a pity to miss out on enjoying so many beautiful plants at close quarters when they're following each other thick and fast.

Florists seldom offer as wide a variety of roses as you might grow in your own garden. These two are 'Bonica' and 'Leonardo da Vinci'.

Early summer

The time of year when spring spills over into summer is one of lushness and abundance in most gardens. Nothing yet looks tired, and there are plenty of flowers to pick. They seem to arrange themselves, with inspiration staring you in the face.

Early summer is when perennials come into their own. Most annuals have not yet reached their peak, but easy herbaceous plants such as hardy geraniums, peonies, perennial poppies, catmints (*Nepeta*), alliums, alstroemeria and *Iris sibirica* are everywhere; roses and clematis are getting well under way; and with

luck there will still be a little residual colour from earlier cottage-garden perennials such as aquilegias and *Centaurea montana*. Wildflowers are becoming plentiful too, with ox-eye daisies (*Leucanthemum vulgare*), foxgloves and many pretty grasses clamouring for a place in your vase.

With so much choice, it's best to be selective each time you go out to gather flowers. Decide on a colour scheme and stick to it, without trying to cram in too great a diversity of material. Soften strong colours with plenty of airy, fresh green flowers; *Alchemilla mollis* and *Tellima grandiflora* are ideal for this

role. They also combine well with soft blues, pastel pinks and whites or stronger, more vivid colours such as the magenta and black of *Geranium* 'Patricia' or the orange of Welsh poppies (*Meconopsis cambrica*) or geums, especially when contrasted with the deep violet-blue of irises, aquilegias and *Centaurea montana*.

Some summer bulbs for cutting

Agapanthus 'Jack's Blue'	Gladiolus communis subsp. byzantinus
Allium cristophii	Gladiolus murielae
Allium sphaerocephalon	Hedychium densiflorum
Allium tuberosum	Lilium regale
Eucomis bicolor	Triteleia laxa 'Koningin Fabiola'
Galtonia candicans	Tulbaghia violacea

Summer exuberance looks its best when tempered by strong plant shapes (here, irises, alliums and phlomis), whether in gardens or vases.

Companions all summer long: *Heuchera* 'Pewter Moon' with the long-flowering, shade-tolerant *Geranium* 'Mavis Simpson'.

Two easy summer plants that are equally good for cutting or drying: greater quaking grass (*Briza maxima*) and the bulb *Allium sphaerocephalon*.

Alstroemerias work well with alliums, masking their fading leaves and at the same time providing a colourful partner for the handsome seedheads.

Other valuable members of the early-summer supporting cast include the delicate 'Hattie's pincushion' flowerheads of *Astrantia major* and the rather invasive but attractive grass *Phalaris arundinacea* (known as gardener's garters).

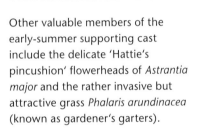

The 'Chelsea chop'

Late spring or early summer – just after the Chelsea Flower Show – is the time for this brutal but handy trick for keeping late summer flowering perennials, such as the larger sedums and Michaelmas daisies, from collapsing under their own weight when fully grown. It also enables you to stagger flowering times, prolonging the season of each variety. Take a pair of shears (and a deep breath: you need to do it just when the plants are looking their most promising) and cut back some of the clumps by about half. They will recover, and will put out new, bushy growth.

Don't forget

After they have bloomed, prune shrubs that flower in late spring and early summer, such as philadelphus, weigela, deutzia and lilac. Cutting out some of the old branches makes space for new growth to flower in the next few years.

Grasses for cutting

Phalaris is by no means the only grass that's good with cut flowers in summer. Grasses can make a useful contribution to your foliage collection for much of the year, with colours ranging from bronze and red to gold and greyish blue. Many have stiff stems, useful for structure in arrangements, and the range of textures and shapes is extraordinary. Leaves range from the wiry threads of blue *Festuca glauca* and amber *Carex buchananii* to the translucent ribbons of Bowles's golden grass (*Milium effusum* 'Aureum'). Flowers include bottlebrushes (*Pennisetum*), dangling lockets (*Briza maxima, Chasmanthium latifolium*), powder-puffs (*Lagurus ovatus*), drooping tassels (*Carex pendula*) and the huge, feathery plumes of pampas grass (*Cortaderia selloana*). Annual *Hordeum jubatum* is a distinctive, easy-to-grow barley with whiskery hairs that look their best when they are caught by low sunshine.

Late-summer drama

It's all too easy for a cutting garden to give up the ghost in late summer. Midsummer classics such as roses and lupins are over, the spring novelty of gardening has worn off, and plants can begin to look tired. You need to have a few tricks up your sleeve to keep the garden going and to give you flowers to cut as summer turns to autumn.

Don't forget

Flowers at the back of a clump, or in shade lower down, may be less advanced and last longer when cut than more obvious stems.

Prevention is better …

The weather can be just as capricious in summer as at any other season, and plants are more vulnerable to extremes of wind, drought or heavy rain while they are growing fast, making soft new leaves and in some cases big flowers. Support helps prevent damage. Twiggy branches are invaluable: it's easy to push a few into the ground around clumps that could fall over when fully grown. Do this when the plants are still small. (*See also* page 42.)

Dahlia 'Bishop of Llandaff', here complemented by a purple-leaved sedum, is attractive for its sumptuous red flowers and its dark leaves.

With its pure, saturated colour, *Lobelia cardinalis* 'Queen Victoria' (seen here with miscanthus) will steal the show if given a rich, moist soil.

Summer fragrance

Many fragrant plants reach their peak at this time of year: scented lilies such as *Lilium regale* capture the very essence of summer, along with roses, philadelphus, jasmine, stocks (*Matthiola*), honeysuckle (*Lonicera*), tobacco plants (*Nicotiana*), pinks (*Dianthus*) and many more. All of these are lovely to bring indoors, but in terms of sheer value for space you can't beat sweet peas, which actually thrive on being cut. Choose the old-fashioned, highly scented varieties of *Lathyrus odoratus*, as some modern seed strains have big, beguiling flowers but little scent. Look out for 'Cupani', 'Matucana', 'Painted Lady' and 'Incense Mix'. It's best to sow seeds in autumn so the plants have time to form a strong root system, then harden them off in spring before planting them out. Give them something to climb up: a wigwam of tall, twiggy hazel branches is ideal, but canes and string work too. Water well, dead-head, and keep picking regularly to encourage more flowers.

Dahlias are a winner – bright and bold and real value for money if you grow them well and dead-head as the flowers fade. Plant them in spring, in rich soil, provide support (*see* page 42) and plenty of water, and you'll have dramatic flowers for weeks. The same applies to zinnias – tender annuals grown from seed. They don't like a wet summer but are so riotous when the weather is in their favour that they're worth a try.

Don't sow them until late spring when the weather warms up, and don't let the growing plants get pot bound or hungry. An equally flamboyant late-summer perennial is *Lobelia cardinalis* 'Queen Victoria' and its many richly coloured relatives in reds, pinks and purples. For late-summer violet-blue to sing out among the reds and yellows, both in borders and in vases, the prominent spikes of *Salvia × superba* are ideal.

Sweet peas are good mixers and complement many other summer flowers. Their partner here is the stiff-stemmed *Verbena bonariensis*.

Verbena rigida provides rich colour for a long summer season. Here it has found a perfect companion in the tobacco plant *Nicotiana* 'Lime Green'.

Plants for summer scents

Dianthus
Gladiolus murielae
Jasminum officinale
Lathyrus odoratus
Lilium regale
Lonicera periclymenum 'Serotina'
Nicotiana sylvestris
Philadelphus
Polianthes tuberosa
Rosa

Don't forget

Dead-heading is critical when plants are at their peak in summer (see page 43) – and can be a real pleasure on a balmy summer evening!

Home-grown flowers beautifully arranged can be a thoughtful and very personalized way of making a celebration a truly special occasion. Don't feel daunted because you think flowers are best left to the professionals. The secret of growing your own is not to try to copy the materials and techniques of formal floristry, but to remind yourself of what you can offer that a florist's shop cannot: a wide variety of sparkling-fresh, natural garden flowers, at a huge cost saving.

Generous planting

Substantial quantities of bought flowers certainly don't come cheap, but by growing your own flowers you will be able to produce enough that are sufficiently bold to make a real impact – even in a large space for a big party or wedding – without counting the pounds. By planting generously, you can also ensure a much wider range of plant material to choose from when the time comes to gather and arrange the flowers for the big day. Be daring and include in your plans some

Choose the right flowers to match their setting.

① *Verbena bonariensis* and euphorbia in a low table decoration.

② A pedestal needs flowers with presence: delphiniums are ideal.

unusual flowers that a florist might not consider sufficiently reliable. They'll probably work – and steal the show – but if they're slow to appear, or have flowered too early, you'll have others in reserve to fall back on.

Table flowers

Flowers for table decorations need to compress maximum interest into minimal space. There must be room for all the other table necessities, and flower arrangements should be kept low so as not to block sight-lines across the table. One approach is to choose flowers with intricate detailing that may not often be seen at close range.

A conversation piece for spring might be unusual primulas in simple, elegant black or terracotta pots: auriculas (*Primula auricula*) or the finely detailed *Primula* Gold-laced Group offer something quite special and different. *Geranium clarkei* 'Kashmir White' and *Geranium pratense* 'Mrs

Kendall Clark' are beautiful as cut flowers in small, dainty arrangements, where the intricate veining on the petals can be examined in detail. Striking patterns and colours are to be found in many violas – both named varieties, such as *Viola sororia* 'Freckles' or *Viola* 'Irish Molly', and exciting self-sown variants that you find in the garden by chance. And don't overlook the potential of pretty leaves, like those of compact ferns, summer jasmine, silvery-purple heucheras, small-leaved ivies (lovely trailing along a table top) and *Azara microphylla* 'Variegata'.

Say it with flowers

There is a historic tradition of associating particular flowers with messages and symbolic meanings. Many of the flowers in the lexicon are traditional, easy-to-grow garden varieties. For example, forget-me-nots are said to represent true love, peonies a happy marriage. Lavender expresses devotion, rosemary remembrance, violets virtue. Choosing at least some flowers according to what they represent can be a charming way to personalize flowers to celebrate a special occasion.

Hosta and *Alchemilla mollis* combine well as an understated foil for roses.

Autumn

As the days grow shorter and nights chillier, there's a strong compulsion to keep summer colour going as long as possible, both in the garden and indoors. With regular dead-heading and a few cleverly chosen late-season perennials, it's perfectly possible to keep on picking flowers pretty well into winter, but remember that autumn also has its very own non-flowery delights, such as berries, seedheads and glowing foliage colour. Be sure to make the most of these. The garden, rather than the florist's shop, is the best place to find them.

A variety of fruits are used here together with ivy flowers in a colourful autumn arrangement.

Late-season flowers

In traditional gardens, herbaceous borders often don't reach their peak until autumn, with a mass of Michaelmas daisies, rudbeckias, golden rod (*Solidago*) and Japanese anemones (*Anemone × hybrida* and *Anemone hupehensis* var. *japonica*) boosting the lingering summer flowers. Gardening styles have changed, but it's still a good idea to plan some colourful perennials with autumn in mind, especially if you're gardening for cut flowers. In a good year, dahlias, cosmos, tender salvias and other frost-sensitive plants may go on flowering well into autumn, but if an early cold spell should cut their performance short it's good to have some hardier flowers to carry the torch for a few more weeks.

Certain summer perennials, such as red valerian (*Centranthus ruber*), heleniums and catmint (*Nepeta*), will flower again now if they were cut back after their summer show, and if you've planted some late-blooming shrubs and perennials among them, your border or cutting garden will have a whole new season of colourful flowers to offer. Aim for a mixture of shapes, heights and textures: sedums (flat and fairly low), eupatoriums (tall, fluffy), *Aconitum carmichaelii* (tall, upright) and

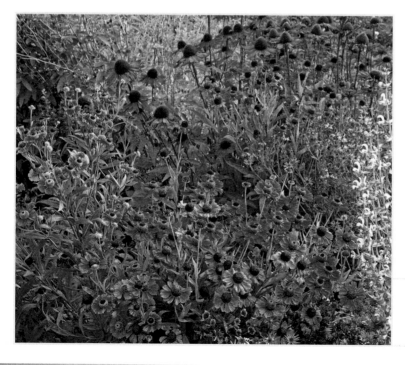

Good plants for late-season colour

Aconitum carmichaelii
Aster amellus 'Veilchenkönigin'
Chrysanthemum
Dahlia
Penstemon
Perovskia atriplicifolia
Physalis alkekengi
Rudbeckia

A colourful mixed autumn border with orange-red heleniums and *Echinacea purpurea,* with their bright pink ruff and distinctive brown cones.

Caryopteris × *clandonensis* (low, bushy) make a good mixture for a sunny bed. Another useful shrub is *Perovskia atriplicifolia*, with upright, silvery-white stems that create a haze of violet-blue when the flowers are open and for some time afterwards.

Gardeners in search of something rather unusual could also try some of the many wonderful and robust autumn-flowering perennials that have in recent years become more widely available with the fashion for prairie-style planting. Examples of these include the little-known but indestructible ironweed (*Vernonia arkansana*) and the lovely, unseasonally fresh-looking tall white daisy *Leucanthemella serotina*. In semi-shady spots with rich soil, try one of several good cultivars of *Actaea simplex*, whose fragrant, late-season bottlebrush flowers are preceded by a mound of delicately divided, deep-purple foliage all summer.

Ornamental seedheads

Until comparatively recently, most gardeners regarded seedheads as something untidy that had to be cut off without delay. But first flower arrangers and then gardeners came to appreciate the value of this long-lasting structural feature, and now it's hard to think how either group managed without them. Seedheads are also valuable for garden wildlife, providing food for

Decorative seedheads for arrangements

There's great variety and interest to be found in seedheads, many of which are ideal for cutting. Gather and dry them at the right time, and they'll last all winter.

Chinese lanterns (*Physalis alkekengi*).

Miss Willmott's ghost (*Eryngium giganteum*).

Opium poppy (*Papaver somniferum*).

finches and other seed-eating birds, and winter shelter for tiny insects.

Not all seedheads are long-lasting in the garden. Those of some pretty summer grasses, such as *Hordeum jubatum* and the quaking grass *Briza maxima*, must be gathered and dried for indoor use while they're in peak condition as they soon shatter. Eryngiums, echinops, alliums and opium poppies (*Papaver somniferum*) also remain in good condition when dried, but eventually deteriorate if left exposed to the weather. Other plants, such as teasels (*Dipsacus fullonum*), honesty (*Lunaria*), phlomis, *Digitalis lutea* and certain grasses, have seedheads that last

An autumn garland

When flowers are becoming scarcer and shortening days make it more difficult to appreciate plants in the garden, try making a simple decorative garland, with home-grown material, to cheer up the house. Hops and other seedheads, berries, fruits and dried flowers can all be used. Bind them together with natural jute twine or raffia and hang the garland over a window or doorway.

through the winter. But even these tough ones can become discoloured or damaged outside, so dry some for indoors while they are still in good condition. Choose a dry, sunny day and cut selectively, leaving some of each kind standing in prominent places as a winter feature for both you and the birds to enjoy outside.

The subtle foliage of evergreen *Eucalyptus gunnii* comes into its own as a backdrop for flamboyant flowers like this *Dahlia* 'Witteman's Superba'.

Who says you need flowers to make an exciting arrangement? Autumn berries and fruits come in almost every colour under the sun, and in some curious shapes too.

Clerodendrum trichotomum var. fargesii.

Spindle (*Euonymus europaeus*).

Callicarpa bodinieri var. *giraldii* 'Profusion'.

Autumn fruits

Bunches of berries glowing in low sunshine are among the highlights of the autumn garden. Many berrying shrubs and trees are equally valuable for cutting – but, just as with seedheads, try to leave some to feed the birds later on. It's also a good idea to have some of the kinds of berries that birds tend to leave until last – such as guelder rose (*Viburnum opulus*), skimmia, aucuba and butcher's broom (*Ruscus aculeatus*). These will provide welcome splashes of warm red in the garden through the winter, and for use in Christmas arrangements for the house, particularly if the birds have pinched all your holly berries!

If you have space to grow them, you can create some unusual effects with branches cut from autumn-berrying shrubs. Some that are better known for red berries are also available in yellow-fruited forms: holly, yew and guelder rose all have cultivars with yellow berries, and pyracantha berries come in yellow or orange as well as red. Blue or purple berries seem rather more outlandish. The deciduous shrub *Callicarpa bodinieri* has clusters of small berries in a wonderful shade of mauve, while those of the low-growing evergreen *Viburnum davidii* are turquoise-blue. *Clerodendrum trichotomum* var. *fargesii* also has turquoise berries, especially striking

because each one sits in the centre of a star-shaped, bright pinkish-red calyx. Spindles *Euonymus europaeus* and *Euonymus planipes* have dazzling fruits that open a shocking-pink calyx to reveal the bright orange seeds. All these are well worth bringing inside to admire close up.

With a few exceptions (such as rowan berries), most fruiting shrubs and trees hang on to their berries until at least mid-autumn, giving you several weeks of gathering them and/or enjoying them in the garden before cold weather drives hungry birds in to feed on them. For fruit to make a large-scale impact, hawthorn cultivars (*Crataegus*), pyracantha, cotoneaster and crab apples (*Malus*) are among the most widely planted.

Compact plants

There are several compact fruiting shrubs, including *Skimmia japonica* 'Red Riding Hood', *Ruscus aculeatus*, and the dwarf form of the guelder rose, *Viburnum opulus* 'Compactum'. In restricted spaces, don't forget that some non-shrubby plants have showy berries: *Arum italicum* and long-lasting *Iris foetidissima*, both with orange-red berries, can be tucked into almost any odd little corner. For black berries on a diminutive plant, grow *Ophiopogon planiscapus* 'Nigrescens', whose fruiting stems last all winter and can be cut to partner early-spring bulbs.

Where ground space is tight, climbing plants are always a useful option. Those that bear berries include *Vitis vinifera* 'Purpurea' (small purple fruits) and *Ampelopsis brevipedunculata* (blue, purple and turquoise berries).

Something of the short-lived beauty of autumn leaves, such as beech, oak, rowan and *Cotinus*, can be preserved by using glycerine. Instead of turning dry and crisp, the leaves become pliable and will last almost indefinitely. Cut healthy stems, condition them (*see page 40*), and then stand them in a tall container in a solution of 1 part glycerine to 2 parts freshly boiled water, about 10cm (4in) deep. Leave the stems in a cool place, and in a few weeks the solution will have replaced the water in the plant cells.

Foliage for cutting

The garden has the edge over the florist's shop, particularly when it comes to foliage. If you have space for a mixed border and a few shrubs, you'll be able to grow a wide range of leaves of every colour, shape, size and texture to put with cut flowers. Foliage in the garden opens up a whole new realm beyond the often dull greenery that goes with bought flowers – especially if it is fragrant.

Trees and shrubs

Woody plants tend to provide the best foliage for flower arrangements, partly because they offer a huge range of material, from branches of newly opened oak leaves or purple beech for grand arrangements to tiny sprays of hebe or thyme foliage for a table posy. They also provide a valuable supporting framework in vases, reducing the need for floristry props such as pinholders, wire and florist's foam. You don't have to have a big garden to be sure of a supply of foliage. Many shrubs with very useful leaves are compact and easy to grow in small spaces, and some will double up as hedging or wall shrubs.

Aim for a wide range of foliage colours. Silver leaves, such as those of grey hebes or the tough *Brachyglottis* Dunedin Group 'Sunshine', are flattering to many flower colours. The small evergold leaves of *Lonicera nitida* 'Baggesen's Gold' make a pleasing partner for deep-blue and purple flowers, while purple and bronze foliage complements red and orange shades. The best purple-leaved plant, being both evergreen and compact, is *Pittosporum tenuifolium* 'Tom Thumb', but there are several larger deciduous shrubs with good dark foliage, such as cultivars of *Cotinus*, elders (*Sambucus*) and *Physocarpus opulifolius* 'Diabolo'.

Green-and-white variegated leaves are a must for giving a visual lift to their vase companions. *Euonymus fortunei* 'Silver Queen' is one of the best for this,

at all times of the year. Very tough once established, it can be trained up a wall or fence to save space. It works equally well in large and small arrangements. White- or cream-variegated evergreens with smaller leaves include the slow-growing variegated box *Buxus sempervirens* 'Elegantissima', and the dainty *Azara microphylla* 'Variegata'.

Herbaceous plants

An ever-increasing number of perennials are grown for their leaves. Hostas and heucheras are two of the most popular, each with hundreds of cultivars. Hosta leaves come in a range of sizes and shapes, and may be yellow, blue-grey or variegated as well as green. Heucheras are more versatile, being evergreen and less prone to slug damage – though they can be victims of vine weevil. Cultivar names such as 'Obsidian', 'Marmalade', 'Lime Rickey', 'Silver Scrolls', 'Pewter Moon' and 'Amethyst Myst' reflect the enormous range of leaf colour. The dainty flowers, mostly in shades of white, pink or green and with wiry stems, make useful filler material in small arrangements. For the best performance, grow heucheras in well-drained, humus-rich soil and divide the clumps frequently. They need some sunshine to produce the best leaf colour.

For some perennials and shrubs whose fragrant foliage will add another dimension to any indoor arrangement, *see* box (right).

Growing a wide variety of foliage inspires creative plant partnerships.

① *Brachyglottis* Dunedin Group 'Sunshine' and *Lonicera nitida* 'Baggesen's Gold'.

② *Cotinus coggygria* 'Royal Purple' with *Jasminum officinale* 'Argenteovariegatum'.

③ *Hosta* 'Bright Lights' and *Heuchera villosa*.

Plants with fragrant foliage

Agastache rugosa	*Melissa officinalis*
Aloysia citrodora	*Mentha pulegium*
Calamintha nepeta	*Monarda*
Hyssopus officinalis	*Myrtus communis*
Juniperus communis 'Compressa'	*Origanum vulgare* 'Aureum'
Laurus nobilis	*Pelargonium* 'Graveolens'
Lavandula angustifolia	*Rosmarinus officinalis*

Winter

Early winter can be a bleak time in the cutting garden. The last of the jewel-like flowers of autumn usually succumb to frosts as the days get ever shorter, and the best autumn leaf colour has passed. But as leaves fall from deciduous trees and shrubs, garden landscapes change, colourful stems are revealed, and structural evergreens that have played second fiddle for half the year re-emerge as key players. Make the most of these in the house too, partnering them with bright berries and seedheads.

Skimmia, variegated holly and ivy support perfect blooms of Christmas rose (*Helleborus niger*), all resulting in a subtly beautiful winter display.

For a time, indoor arrangements revolve mainly around evergreen foliage, coloured stems, fruits and seedheads (*see* pages 57–9), with few if any flowers to be gathered. It feels somehow right, though, to have these in the house when days are shortest, as a kind of celebration of the year that is ending. Then, once midwinter is past and the days begin to lengthen again, tiny and oh-so-welcome signs of spring slowly begin to gather pace as late-winter bulbs and blossom get into gear for the coming season.

Stem colour

The garden landscape in winter can be brightened amazingly by choosing plants with interesting bark. Many of the most popular, such as birches and paperbark maple (*Acer griseum*), are features to be admired from the windows rather than to be cut for the house, but some shrubs do have coloured stems that make good cutting material.

Several species of dogwood, in particular, have cultivars grown partly for the colours of their bare young stems. Brightest and most suitable for smaller gardens are cultivars of the native dogwood; *Cornus sanguinea* 'Midwinter Fire' is the most popular, but you may also come across 'Winter Beauty'. *Cornus alba* also has cultivars with bright young stems: red in *Cornus alba* 'Elegantissima' and 'Sibirica Variegata', both of which also have variegated leaves that make them

Frosted seedheads and grasses make their own winter arrangement, to be admired from a window.

Winter opportunists

Winter jasmine (*Jasminum nudiflorum*), the winter-flowering viburnums and the winter-flowering cherry tree (*Prunus × subhirtella* 'Autumnalis') belong to a small but very welcome group of plants that take advantage of any mild winter weather to burst enthusiastically into bloom, providing cheering little sprays of flowers to bring indoors. They can go on doing this for months, their flowers seemingly ruined by frost one week, only for more to emerge the next. Not all last well in water, but winter jasmine will continue to open new flowers indoors, staying fresh for several days.

Winter fragrance is at its best when it takes you by surprise on a mild day in the garden, but it can work well indoors too. In a warm room, the scent from even a sprig or two of perfumed blossom can be astonishing: make the most of it before it fades.

Sarcococca confusa: a compact, shade-tolerant evergreen.

Chimonanthus praecox has the richest, spiciest scent of all.

Faintly scented but glowing: *Hamamelis × intermedia* 'Diane'.

Mahonia × media 'Winter Sun' usually flowers before Christmas.

attractive all year. *Cornus alba* 'Kesselringii' has darker, blackish-purple stems, while those of the vigorous *Cornus sericea* 'Flaviramea' and 'Bud's Yellow' are gold.

The coral-bark maple, *Acer palmatum* 'Sango-kaku', is a good garden plant with pinkish-red stems, and several willow cultivars also bear colourful young shoots. Those of *Salix alba* var. *vitellina* 'Britzensis' glow burnished orange, while *Salix daphnoides* 'Aglaia' has violet stems.

Lastly, consider *Rubus thibetanus*, which matures to form a fountain of arching, ghostly-white stems – most attractive. But wear stout gloves when you cut it, as it is very prickly.

Winter flowers

The few bulbs and perennials that flower on the coldest, darkest days are all the more valuable because they're scarce. Snowdrops (*Galanthus*) are lovely to bring indoors, opening out to display their green inner markings. Pull each stem gently from the clump, rather than cutting it. The flowers are good company for the very hardy *Cyclamen coum*.

Hellebores are another winter favourite. The Christmas rose (*Helleborus niger*) is special but can be tricky to grow. Green-flowered *Helleborus foetidus* is an easier plant for odd corners. The Lenten rose (*Helleborus × hybridus*) has become a connoisseur's plant, with many prized dark, spotted or double varieties, but a generous patch of ordinary pink and white ones at the back of a border is just as pleasing.

Remember to sear the stems of hellebores (*see* page 40); they also look good with their flowerheads floating in water (*see* page 18).

Scented plants

Fragrant plants are such a joy to bring into the house on wintry days. Especially welcome in the early days of winter, when little else is in flower, is the large evergreen shrub *Mahonia japonica*, whose sprays of yellow flowers have a fresh perfume similar to that of lily-of-the-valley. Some varieties of *Mahonia × media* are scented, too. Also flowering in early winter are the evergreens *Elaeagnus × ebbingei* and *Elaeagnus pungens*, useful foliage plants for large arrangements, with scented, tiny flowers hidden beneath their leaves.

A recipe for winter cheer: the bright, bare white stems of *Rubus thibetanus* with *Cornus sanguinea* 'Winter Beauty' and *Cornus alba* 'Sibirica'.

One of the most evocative scents after midwinter is that of wintersweet (*Chimonanthus praecox*). You need only pick a few twigs to fill a whole room with a spicy, warm, sweet fragrance and they should last for several days. A few sprigs of sarcococca's late-winter blossom also really pack a punch.

Hamamelis mollis is reputedly the most fragrant of the witch hazels, though some *Hamamelis × intermedia* varieties are more striking to look at, some with unseasonably warm colours, like the rich red of 'Diane' or the orange of 'Jelena'.

Ivies

Ivies should find a place in every garden for their great value as winter greenery. They are among the most long-suffering of plants, tolerant of heavy shade, drought and neglect.

Cut lengths of some of the young shoots and use them to trail prettily along from a low table decoration

Fragrance indoors for the darkest days of winter: easy-to-grow *Narcissus papyraceus* and prepared hyacinths.

work with and useful for holding everything else together.

Make use of the berries too, either when green or ripe and black. Found only on mature plants, they ripen much later than nearly all other fruits, which is handy for both flower arrangers and garden birds.

Forcing bulbs

Growing bulbs to enjoy their colour and fragrance indoors, some weeks before they flower outside, has long been a popular practice. Some bulbs are sold specially prepared for early flowering by artificially speeding up their seasonal cycle.

Prepared hyacinth bulbs, for flowering in midwinter, are available in early autumn. Plant them in pots of damp multipurpose compost as soon as you can. They need cold and darkness for several weeks to develop their roots, so bury the pots in a bed outdoors or keep them in a dark, cool shed or garage. When the flower buds have pushed through the surface of the compost, bring the pots into a light but fairly cool place indoors. When you see colour on the buds, move the pots to their flowering position.

There are several fragrant narcissi, notably *Narcissus papyraceus* (known as 'Paper White') and 'Soleil d'Or', which need no cold period to start them off and take only about six weeks from planting to flowering, so it's possible to have them in flower from late autumn.

in the same way that you might use jasmine or clematis in summer. Ivies also work well in Christmas wreaths and garlands, their tough but flexible stems being easy to

Interesting ivies for winter arrangements

Ivies are invaluable in winter, with their variety of leaf shapes and variegations. Use them in Christmas decorations and arrangements, and to partner late-winter bulbs.

Hedera helix 'Glacier'

Hedera helix 'Pedata'

Hedera helix 'Oro di Bogliasco'

Christmas from your garden

With a little advance planning, it's not at all difficult to produce home-grown decorations for Christmas. Making them is not only very therapeutic in the busy run-up to the festive season; it can also be an enjoyable part of that traditional, special pre-Christmas feeling of anticipation.

Christmas greenery and berries

Holly and ivy are the main components of traditional Christmas greenery – both easy garden plants, though holly can be slow to establish and bear fruit. It may be worth sourcing a more mature (though more expensive) shrub if you are in a hurry for berries. Self-fertile *Ilex aquifolium* 'J.C. van Tol' is the one to plant if there are no other

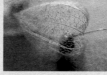

hollies nearby. Many other evergreens are useful for decorating the house at Christmas, and it's especially nice to include some fragrant foliage, for instance rosemary, bay, myrtle, thuja or cypress, if you have them growing in the garden. White-variegated foliage, including *Hedera helix* 'Glacier' or *Euonymus fortunei* 'Silver Queen', is also useful for adding a light touch to a garland or table decoration.

If holly berries are in short supply, you can cheat by using other red berries, perhaps skimmia or cotoneaster, or rose-hips, tied in a bunch with holly leaves and ribbon.

Seedheads

Architectural seedheads sprayed silver, gold or even red make unusual and striking Christmas decorations, either

Creating home-grown decorations can be a really special and enjoyable part of your preparations for Christmas.
① A welcoming wreath for the front door.
② Traditional materials: ivy and mistletoe.
③ Something different: *Eucalyptus gunnii*.

in displays with greenery and berries, or tucked into a garland or wreath. *Eryngium giganteum*, *Echinops*, *Nicandra physalodes* and opium poppies (*Papaver somniferum*) are among the most effective ones to use. The cones from larch or fir trees work well, too. Make sure they are perfectly dry, and spray them outdoors on a still day (it's best to put them in a cardboard box or plastic bag to do this). The seedheads of *Iris foetidissima* need no such adornment: their stiff stems of orange berries are effective in a gold or silver vase, brightening a dim corner.

A Christmas wreath

An original, stylish wreath for the front door can be made in an hour or less using only plant material from the garden. Make a circular frame by winding together several flexible young stems of dogwood or another similar vigorous shrub that produces whippy, unbranched stems. Cover it with greenery such as ivy tendrils and sprigs of bay, myrtle, variegated euonymus or Portugal laurel. Then tie in some colour and sparkle: sprigs of holly or another shrub with red berries, Chinese lanterns, or *Iris foetidissima*, plus some seedheads of honesty or eryngium sprayed silver or gold. Finally, add a hook or a loop of stiff wire to hang it up by, and perhaps a festive bow.

Chinese lanterns

Physalis alkekengi is a rather invasive plant but easy to grow. Its long stems of glowing orange-red lanterns have real impact in the autumn garden and keep their colour well if picked and gently dried (first removing the leaves) before late-autumn rains and frosts spoil them. The individual 'lanterns' are perfect to use as natural Christmas tree decorations, and strings of fine twine hung with them make striking festive garlands. In late winter, look out for 'skeletonized' lanterns: exposed to the weather, the red covering disintegrates to leave a light-as-air seed case like fine lacework. Paint or spray some with gold or silver for delicate and unusual decorations.

Allium seedheads are very decorative sprayed with paint in seasonal colours.

Recommended plants for cutting

Recommending the best flowers and foliage for cutting is a nigh-impossible task. Everyone has their favourites, and the possibilities are endless, embracing tens of thousands of garden plants. This A–Z directory aims to include something for everyone. The selection ranges from 'old faithfuls' used by generations of flower arrangers to newly fashionable structural perennials and wildflowers – with, hopefully, a few things you may not have thought of.

A–Z directory

Here you will find a selection of plants for all seasons – and for all purposes, too. Think of the following pages as a basic tool-kit to help you put together beautiful mixed arrangements using flowers and foliage from the garden.

You'll find colourful summer annuals; easy spring bulbs; trusty, long-flowering perennials and foliage shrubs that are dramatic, or subtle, or simply very useful – not to mention berries and seedheads for autumn and winter, and grasses to add texture to arrangements. Many are star performers, while others make great partners for showier blooms. For tips on extending the life of cut flowers and foliage, *see* page 40.

KEY to symbols

In this chapter the following symbols are used to indicate a plant's preferred growing conditions and uses. A rough idea is given as to what each plant's height (H) and spread (S) might be at maturity. Where a range is given, the size may depend on the variety.

Unless otherwise specified, plants are fully hardy and deciduous.

○ prefers/tolerates an open, sunny site

◐ prefers/tolerates some shade

● prefers/tolerates full shade

❄ will survive winter in a sheltered site

❋ always needs protection from frost

♦ prefers/tolerates moist soil

◊ prefers/tolerates dry soil

⇊ needs well-drained soil

pH↓ prefers/tolerates acidic soil

pH↑ prefers/tolerates alkaline soil

pH← prefers/tolerates neutral soil

🍂 needs humus-rich soil

❖ season of main interest (e.g. flowers, foliage, stems, berries)

Acanthus spinosus
Bear's breeches
○ ◐ ⇊ ❖ LATE SUMMER
H and S 1m (40in)

With long-lasting, architectural flower spikes, bear's breeches is as imposing in arrangements as in the garden. It dries well too, and has striking prickly leaves. The plant is drought-tolerant, deep-rooted and almost indestructible. It is hard to move, so think carefully about the right spot for it before you plant.

Achillea filipendulina 'Gold Plate'
○ ◊ ⇊ ❖ LATE SUMMER
H 1.5m (5ft) S 1m (40in)

The horizontal plates of flowers on stiff stems make achilleas classic architectural plants for both borders and vases. The flowerheads dry well if picked when fresh. 'Gold Plate' is the one for impact in large arrangements. A. 'Summerwine' (burgundy red) and A. 'Terracotta' are smaller. Give achilleas support in a border and split clumps every other year to keep them vigorous.

Agapanthus 'Jack's Blue'
○ ⇊ ❖ LATE SUMMER to AUTUMN
H 1.2m (4ft) S 45cm (18in)

It seems to be widely agreed that 'Jack's Blue' is one of the best of the numerous cultivars of agapanthus, fairly hardy and imposing with large, deep violet-blue flowers on straight stems. If you want white flowers, go for A. 'Polar Ice' and for smaller spaces choose the more compact cultivar 'Lilliput', which also does well in a pot. All do best in a sunny, sheltered spot with fertile soil that does not dry out easily.

Agastache Anise hyssop
○ ⇊ ❖ LATE SUMMER to AUTUMN
H 90cm (3ft) S 45cm (18in)

These stiff, aromatic perennials have mint-like vertical flower spikes that are useful as dried seedheads as well as fresh flowers. They are also very wildlife-friendly, with nectar for insects in summer and seeds for small birds in winter. A. 'Blue Fortune' (shown above) is one of the best blues. Other agastaches come in pink, orange and white; some are hardier than others.

Alchemilla mollis Lady's mantle
○ ◑ ♦ ↓↓ ❖ EARLY SUMMER to EARLY AUTUMN
H 60cm (24in) S 75cm (30in)

Whether in the garden or in a vase, alchemilla's role is as a foil to other plants that contrast in colour and/or texture. Use it in small to medium-sized arrangements for its frothy mass of tiny, acid-green flowers or for its pleated, scalloped leaves, so pretty-looking when spangled with raindrops. Cut the plants back to the ground after flowering, and a crop of fresh new foliage will appear.

Allium hollandicum
○ ↓↓ ❖ LATE SPRING to EARLY SUMMER
H 75cm (30in) S 10cm (4in)

Also known as *A. aflatunense*, this is probably the best all-purpose garden allium and the earliest of the larger-flowered varieties. The brightly coloured flowerheads are not too heavy to cope with wind and rain, nor too cumbersome to use easily in mixed arrangements. In conditions that suit it, it will go on for years, forming impressive groups if you encourage self-sown seedlings. The seedheads last well in the garden, and tend to stay on the plant longer than those of *A. cristophii* (see panel, right).

Allium

Allium schubertii, dramatic fresh or dried.

Stars of Chelsea

The main flowering season for these ornamental members of the onion family begins in late spring, around the time of the Chelsea Flower Show, where they are always much in evidence. This is with good reason: alliums have a unique role in the garden, with their distinctive 'drumstick' shape making a very positive, architectural contribution to planting schemes and flower arrangements alike.

The more intricately structured varieties, such as *Allium cristophii* and *A. schubertii*, make beautiful and long-lasting single specimens, fresh or dried, in a slender vase with a heavy base. And don't forget the

Alliums come in various shapes, sizes and colours. Left: *Allium sphaerocephalon.* Below left: *Allium cernuum.* Below right: *Allium tuberosum.*

humble leek, which will make a splendidly statuesque flowerhead if left to grow for a second season. The most familiar alliums have purple or mauve flowers, but there are scores of species and cultivars spanning a colour range that also includes white, yellow, blue and pink.

Where to grow them

A drawback with most alliums is that the leaves die off just as the flowers are at their best. For cutting, plant them in rows in a vegetable patch or an allotment, or in a sunny mixed border, where they can borrow some cover-up foliage from neighbouring low shrubs or from herbaceous plants such as hardy geraniums.

GOOD ALLIUM VARIETIES

Allium atropurpureum – Moody dark maroon, domed flowerheads; an attractive vase companion for silver, blue and lime green.

A. caeruleum – Compact flowerheads of clear blue. Likes a dry, sunny spot.

A. cernuum (see left) – Small heads of attractively nodding flowers. Good value for picking.

A. cristophii – Large, airy, silvery-mauve globes. Lovely if dried when fresh.

A. hollandicum (see far left).

A. nigrum – Well-shaped, greenish-white domes on tall stems, but the seedheads don't last.

A. schubertii (see above) – Pale purple flowers on stalks of differing lengths.

A. sphaerocephalon (see left) – Useful late-flowering allium with small, dense oval heads on long stems. Tough and easy. Good for drying.

A. tuberosum (Chinese chives, garlic chives) (see left) – Fresh, pretty white flowers in late summer, with edible leaves and durable seedheads.

Alstroemeria Peruvian lily
○ ◗ ‼ ❖ SUMMER

H to 1m (40in) S 90cm (3ft)

Their extended season of colourful, long-lasting cut flowers has traditionally made alstroemerias popular in floristry, and they are easy perennials in the garden once established. Take care to minimize disturbance to the roots when planting them out, though. *A. ligtu* hybrids used to be the standard variety to grow from seed, but many other cultivars and seed strains are now available. Shown above is *A.* 'Friendship'.

Anemone coronaria
○ ‼ ❖ SPRING

H 30–40cm (12–16in) S 15cm (6in)

A popular cut flower for its deep, velvety colours, *A. coronaria* is not expensive to buy as dried tubers and can be grown in containers or beds, under cover or outdoors. Choose between the single flowers of the De Caen Group or the doubles known as Saint Bridgid Group. Both types are available either as mixtures or in single colour strains such as 'Die Braut' ('The Bride'; white) and 'Mister Fokker' (shown above).

Anemone × hybrida 'Honorine Jobert' Japanese anemone
◗ ◗ ‼ ❖ LATE SUMMER to AUTUMN

H and S 1.5m (5ft)

This is a great plant for autumn, bringing a real breath of fresh air to tired borders with its white flowers. The bobbly seedheads are attractive too. It is good in partial shade, and although it prefers a moist, rich soil it will tolerate dry sites. *A. hupehensis* 'Hadspen Abundance' is one of several more compact autumn anemones in shades of pink. All are long-lived and long-flowering.

Antirrhinum majus Snapdragon
○ ✵ ‼ ❖ SUMMER to EARLY AUTUMN

H and S 20–60cm (8–24in)

Usually sold as annuals, snapdragons are in fact short-lived perennials and may survive several winters. Happy in pots, they come in numerous cultivars and a wide range of colours. The taller types in deep shades, such as rich reds, are the most useful for cutting and make impressive plants. Good varieties include 'Black Prince' (shown above) and 'Night and Day'. Pick flowers regularly to keep plants productive.

Aquilegia Columbine
○ ◗ ‼ ❖ SPRING to EARLY SUMMER

H 30–60cm (12–24in) S 45cm (18in)

Although they last only a few days in water, aquilegias have other qualities that make them good for cutting: an intricate flower shape, a convenient flowering season between bulbs and summer perennials, and a tendency to self-sow. Partner the deep-blue ones with golden marjoram, ox-eye daisies, orange *Meconopsis cambrica* and *Tellima grandiflora*. Shown above is *A. bertolonii*.

Aster 'Little Carlow'
○ ◗ ❖ EARLY AUTUMN

H and S 90cm (3ft)

Many Michaelmas daisies are lovely both in the garden and for cutting. *A.* 'Little Carlow' is a favourite of many gardeners, reliably producing masses of bright lavender-blue flowers that make a real impact. *A.* × *frikartii* 'Mönch' has a very long flowering season starting earlier than most asters, while *A. amellus* 'Veilchenkönigin' ('Violet Queen') is a compact, deep-purple one for the front of a border. All these are resistant to mildew, which can plague Michaelmas daisies, especially in dry soils.

Briza maxima
Greater quaking grass
○◐◇‡‡ ❖ SUMMER
H 30–60cm (12–24in) S 20cm (8in)

One of the prettiest and easiest of grasses, this annual quaking grass has locket-shaped flowerheads suspended from thread-like stems so fine they sway in the slightest breeze. The graceful stems enhance any arrangement. The shiny flowerheads catch the light beautifully and also dry very well if gathered when fresh. They will eventually disintegrate if left outdoors, but leave a few to ripen and you may find seedlings for next year. Take care not to weed these out by mistake.

Calendula officinalis Pot marigold
○◐ ❖ SUMMER to EARLY AUTUMN
H 30–60cm (12–24in) S 30cm (12in)

Pot marigolds are among the jolliest of annuals, with their open, fresh faces in shades of orange and yellow. They are also easy to grow and even edible. They are the perfect unpretentious cottage-garden flowers for a simple dark blue or white jug on a kitchen table. Dead-head the plants to ensure a succession of flowers, leaving a few to self-sow at the end of the season.

Campanula lactiflora
Milky bellflower
◐◆◇‡‡ ❖ LATE SUMMER
H 1.5m (5ft) S 60cm (2ft)

This tough but attractive clump-forming perennial is most commonly seen in the reliable violet-blue form, 'Prichard's Variety' (shown above), but also comes in pink and white. All are useful as they flower late in the season. Dead-head for a succession of flowers and support plants with tall, twiggy sticks as they grow. Cut flowers to bring indoors as they begin to open; blooms soon fade if they have been pollinated by insects.

Campanula persicifolia
Peach-leaved bellflower
○◐◑◇‡‡ ❖ SUMMER
H 60–90cm (2–3ft) S 30cm (12in)

A traditional border perennial for flowering alongside roses, C. persicifolia has stiff, straight stems that are good for cutting when the flowers start to open. Blue and white forms are most often seen, but look out for the choice cultivar 'Chettle Charm' (shown above), with white bells whose edges appear to have been dipped in light blue ink. 'Telham Beauty' has larger, blue flowers; 'Powder Puff' has double, creamy-white flowers.

Catananche caerulea
Cupid's dart
○◇‡‡ ❖ LATE SUMMER
H 45cm (18in) S 20cm (8in)

This unusual and drought-tolerant little perennial owes its long season of interest partly to its attractive silvery buds, which eventually burst open in late summer into a mass of flowers that are similar in form to wild hawkweeds or dandelions but in a lovely shade of lavender blue. Stiff, wiry stems make this a good cutting plant. It takes up little space, and is easy to grow in well-drained soil, and quick to flower from seed.

Centaurea cyanus Cornflower
○ ❖ SUMMER to EARLY AUTUMN
H 90cm (3ft) S 45cm (18in)

There's something special about the true, deep blue of the hardy annual wild cornflower. Seed strains in other colours, such as 'Black Ball' (shown above) and 'Red Boy', are just as useful for cutting and in the garden, and perform better than the blue, which tends to fade. Sow in autumn for the sturdiest plants, and support them well as they grow.

Centranthus ruber Red valerian
○ ◑ ◊ ↕ pH←—pH↑ ❖ SUMMER to AUTUMN
H and S 60cm (2ft)

The red, pink or white flowers of this familiar, easy seaside perennial appear at intervals from late spring through to autumn. Grow several plants and you will have flowers continuously if you cut the stems hard back in rotation as the old flowers fade. Allow a stem or two to self-sow and new plants will pop up in odd corners, gravel or paving cracks, but be careful near old walls, where they may take root and damage the masonry.

Cerinthe major 'Purpurascens'
Honeywort
○ ◊ ↕ ❖ SPRING to AUTUMN
H and S 30–60cm (12–24in)

This subtle and sophisticated-looking annual is easy to grow, thriving (and possibly even self-sowing) in dry, sunny gardens. Its curious, moody, purple-blue drooping flowers and silvery-green, semi-succulent foliage are especially good partners for lime green, orange and red. Try combining it with euphorbias, nasturtiums or poppies.

Chionodoxa luciliae
○ ↕ ❖ EARLY SPRING
H 15cm (6in) S 10cm (4in)

Along with the small, early-flowering scillas, chionodoxas are reliable and welcome harbingers of spring, spreading to create pools of blue in a sunny spot. The bulbs can be tucked into borders and under deciduous shrubs and hedges, taking up little space. For a stronger blue, try *C. sardensis*. You might also try *C.* 'Pink Giant' (shown above) or the starry white *C. luciliae* 'Alba'.

Choisya × *dewitteana* 'Aztec Pearl' Mexican orange blossom
○ ◑ ◐ ↕ ❖ LATE SPRING, EARLY AUTUMN
H and S 2.5m (8ft)

With well-shaped, glossy foliage and highly fragrant, white waxy flowers, usually twice a year, this easy evergreen shrub earns its space in a sheltered spot. Cutting flowering shoots for the house helps to keep the bush compact and encourages a second flowering; choisyas also respond to harder pruning if they have become straggly. The similar *C. ternata* 'Sundance' is one of the few shrubs with plain 'evergold' foliage.

Chrysanthemum
○ ◕ ↕ ❖ SUMMER to AUTUMN
H 30–120cm (1–4ft) S 60–90cm (2–3ft)

Chrysanthemums are staples of the floristry trade. This may be a reason not to grow them, but hardy perennial types can be useful for late-autumn colour. Reliable varieties include 'Duchess of Edinburgh' (shown above), 'Emperor of China' (pink) and 'Nantyderry Sunshine' (yellow). Annual chrysanthemums are less well known but ideal for a cutting patch or allotment – easy to grow and hardy enough to sow in autumn.

Clematis × *durandii*
○ ◑ ◐ ↕ ❖ MIDSUMMER to EARLY AUTUMN
H 1.8m (6ft) S 1.5m (5ft)

Many clematis have exquisite flowers that repay the close attention they get in a vase. One of the bluest, this non-clinging hybrid is at home as a bold element of a mixed arrangement, or in a small vase with two or three flowers of other richly coloured clematis varieties. Choose the flowers with the longest stalks, cutting them just as they open. Keep the plant moist and shade its roots to ward off mildew later in the summer.

Consolida ajacis Larkspur
◐◑ ❖ SUMMER
H to 90cm (3ft) S 30cm (12in)

Their elegant form makes larkspurs some of the most useful of hardy annuals, with lovely colours ranging from deep, rich blues, purples and pinks to white (above, Sublime Mixed). Close relatives of delphiniums, they are quite long-lived when cut, and keep their colour well as dried flowers. Sow seeds in late summer or early autumn to flower early the next year, and another batch in spring to flower later. Protect the young plants from slugs and stake taller plants.

Convallaria majalis
Lily-of-the-valley
◑💧🌿 ❖ LATE SPRING
H 25cm (10in) S 30cm (12in)

Many of us remember the fragrance of this classic cottage-garden plant from childhood. It is at its most evocative in small bunches freshly picked for the house, or growing in a sheltered, confined spot with dampish soil and some sunshine to bring out its unmistakable scent. Once established, it makes usefully dense ground cover in the right place, but take care not to let it run unchecked among other plants.

Coreopsis verticillata Tickseed
◐◑≣ ❖ SUMMER
H 45cm (18in) S 30cm (12in)

Strong wiry stems, feathery foliage and a long flowering season earn perennial coreopsis a place in any cutting patch. The species has bright gold flowers, like small single dahlias; the paler, lemon-yellow 'Moonbeam' (shown above) is prettier perhaps, but not as tough. Annual coreopsis (sometimes known as calliopsis) come in various seed strains with plain or bicoloured flowers: red and bronze as well as yellow, usually a mix.

Cornus alba 'Sibirica Variegata'
◐◑💧 ❖ YEAR-ROUND
H and S 2m (6ft)

This is one of the best-value deciduous shrubs, attractive at every season and providing a variety of cutting material all year. Glowing coral-red winter stems produce elegant, white-variegated leaves in spring. The foliage looks attractive all summer, briefly turning shrimp-pink before leaf fall. *C.a.* 'Elegantissima' is similar but more vigorous; *C.a.* 'Spaethii' has gold-variegated leaves. *C. sanguinea* cultivars (like 'Midwinter Fire') have even brighter stems but plain leaves.

Corylus avellana 'Contorta'
Corkscrew hazel
◐◑ ❖ WINTER to SPRING
H and S 3m (10ft)

This crazy, curly version of common hazel is a conversation piece in the garden, as a container specimen, or cut for indoors. Long branches work well in big winter arrangements, or a stem or two can be displayed to great effect in a clear glass vase that shows every twist and turn. Once the leaves are open, as twisted as the stems, the plant looks strange and rather sickly, so keep it out of the spotlight through the summer.

Cosmos bipinnatus
○❀ ❖ SUMMER to AUTUMN
H 1.2m (4ft) S 90cm (3ft)

Fast-growing and elegant, cosmos are excellent annuals to prevent borders looking tired in late summer. Dead-head them and they will flower until the first frosts. For best effect, grow a few plants of a tall variety such as 'Dazzler' (dark pink, shown above) or 'Purity' (white). You can sow cosmos quite late in spring; pinch out the tips to make bushy plants, and keep them growing vigorously until planting out in early summer.

Cotinus coggygria 'Royal Purple' Purple smoke bush
○ ◑ ⍢ ❖ LATE SPRING to AUTUMN
H and S 3m (10ft)

A well-grown purple cotinus is a fine plant, looking its best in the garden when low early-morning or evening sun shines through the rounded, deep purplish-red leaves. It is particularly effective as a foil for reds and other hot colours in arrangements. The leaves will be larger if the shrub is pruned hard in spring, but the feathery flower plumes grow only on old wood. *C.* 'Grace' is robust and more brightly coloured.

Crocosmia 'Lucifer' Montbretia
○ ◑ ◔ ⍢ 🍂 ❖ LATE SUMMER to AUTUMN
H 1.2m (4ft) S 60cm (2ft)

Dazzling red trumpet flowers on tall, stately, arched stems make C. 'Lucifer' a popular crocosmia, though it is just one of many varieties spanning the yellow, red and orange part of the spectrum. In the right spot, the plants should provide bright flowers, structural seedheads and smart, sword-like leaves year after year. Use 'Lucifer' with bold contrasting colours: deep-blue salvias, silver eryngiums and yellow-and-white daisies.

Dahlia 'Bishop of Llandaff'
○ ◔ ⍢ ❖ LATE SUMMER to AUTUMN
H and S 90cm (3ft)

This is probably the gardening world's most popular dahlia; it is hard to fault, with dark, rich foliage making a foil for simple, blood-red flowers adorned only by a ring of small golden stamens. It is easy to grow, too, and relatively hardy for a dahlia, sometimes surviving winter out in the garden. Mulch it in autumn to improve the chances. In the growing season, keep it well fed and watered and support it with stakes.

Daphne bholua
○ ◑ ◔ ⍢ 🍂 ❖ LATE WINTER to SPRING
H 2.5m (8ft) S 1.2m (4ft)

This is one of the best daphnes for a mild, sheltered garden. It is generous with its sweetly fragrant pink flowers, and soon grows tall enough for them to be appreciated at nose level. Plant it near a gateway or beside a path that you use often, including during the winter, so that you can enjoy the scent as well as being reminded to pick small sprigs to bring into the home.

Delphinium
○ ⍢ ❖ SUMMER
H 1.2–2.5m (4–8ft) S 60cm (2ft)

Delphiniums are among the stars of the summer border, and are worthy of the grandest arrangements. More often than not, this is a plant requiring a degree of commitment to grow it successfully. Fertile soil, adequate water, proper staking and slug control will probably all be needed.Good varieties include 'Alice Artindale' (shown above) and the much darker Black Knight Group.

Dianthus barbatus Sweet william
○ ❖ LATE SPRING to EARLY SUMMER
H 60cm (24in) S 45cm (18in)

Sweet williams combine fragrance with distinctive flowers in a mix of rich colours and patterns. Single colours are also available. The plants are perennial, and may go on for years if cut back after flowering, but are traditionally grown as biennials, sown in a cutting bed in early summer to transplant later, in rows or in patches in a border, to flower the following year. Try them with acid-green euphorbias and *Alchemilla mollis*.

Digitalis grandiflora
Yellow foxglove
○◑ ❖ SUMMER
H 60cm (24in) S 30cm (12in)

Many foxgloves are biennial, but this short, pale yellow one, like the taller, smaller-flowered *D. lutea*, is perennial (and often self-sows). Its colour is an easy partner for other plants, good with whites, blues and deep pink. Compact and easy to grow, this is an ideal plant for a cutting patch or the front of a border, usually producing several flower spikes per plant – so you can cut some and leave others to enjoy in the garden.

Dipsacus fullonum Teasel
○◑ ❖ SUMMER to WINTER
H 1.5m (5ft) S 90cm (3ft)

This statuesque biennial wildflower makes an impressive garden plant, attractive to bees and butterflies and providing a winter seed crop irresistible to goldfinches. Stiff, prickly stems make good 'scaffolding' in both fresh and dried arrangements, and the seedheads are useful in Christmas decorations. The plants often self-sow – too generously for some gardeners – but the seedlings are easy to remove when small.

Echinacea purpurea Coneflower
○◑◦⁂ ❖ LATE SUMMER to AUTUMN
H 60–90cm (2–3ft) S 45cm (18in)

Echinaceas are free-flowering plants with elegant, long-lasting flowers. They are good nectar plants for butterflies and bees too, so plant enough to leave some in the garden as well as to cut for the house. *E. purpurea* is unusual in its combination of pink (or white) petals and bronze cone. Old varieties tend to be more reliable than some of the brighter new cultivars, and keep their shape better after flowering.

Echinops Globe thistle
○◑⁂ ❖ LATE SUMMER to AUTUMN
H 1.2m (4ft) S 60cm (2ft)

The spherical, metallic-blue flowerheads of globe thistles are very good for cutting, and for bees, but the thug-like habits of some varieties have given them a bad name. However, compact forms like *E. bannaticus* 'Taplow Blue' (shown above) and *E. ritro* 'Veitch's Blue' are worth growing. Tough and drought-tolerant, they bear unusual flowers in late summer, and often again in late autumn if cut to the ground after flowering. The buds dry well for decorations.

Elaeagnus 'Quicksilver'
○◑◦⁂ ❖ SPRING to AUTUMN
H and S 2m (6ft)

A vigorous grower that will keep you supplied with silver foliage for months, this deciduous shrub can also be trained as an elegant little tree by keeping it pruned, from a young plant, with a clear, straight trunk. The fragrance from the tiny flowers in late spring is delightful. It's a good companion for rich blues and reds in summer, when the new growth has matured a little: young shoots tend to be floppy, but otherwise it cuts well.

Epimedium Barrenwort,
Bishop's mitre
◑◦🍂 ❖ YEAR-ROUND
H 20–30cm (8–12in) S 60cm (24in)

Epimediums are woodland perennials with attractive ground-covering foliage, held on wiry stems, for much of the year. When there is no danger of frost, the leaves can be cut down in late winter to reveal the unfurling stems of the new flowers. Ranging from white through yellow to pink, they seem insignificant in the garden, but they are perfectly formed and look lovely in dainty posies. Shown above is *E. × rubrum*.

Eremurus Foxtail lily
○ ◐ ◊ ‖ ❖ SUMMER

H 1.2–3m (4–10ft) S 60–90cm (2–3ft)

The tall, sleek spikes of foxtail lilies make them ideal candidates for big, dramatic flower arrangements. Grow plenty: they look splendid in the garden and indoors, so you'll want enough for both. They like good, free-draining soil and fairly shallow planting. Colours include orange-apricot E. × isabellinus 'Cleopatra' (shown above) and the lovely cool white E. himalaicus, as well as yellow and pink.

Eryngium giganteum
Miss Willmott's ghost
○ ◐ ◊ ‖ ❖ SUMMER to AUTUMN

H to 90cm (3ft) S 45cm (18in)

This is an invaluable biennial whose stiff stems and shapely (if prickly) flowers add a strong structural element to flower arrangements as well as borders. A deep tap root, developed over two seasons or more, will sustain the plant, even in very dry gardens, until it flowers and dies, leaving a handsome skeleton that may remain intact until autumn. Dry a few newly opened flowerheads for Christmas. It self-sows freely.

Eryngium

Eryngiums for cutting

With their long-lasting architectural flowerheads, similar to thistles, in steely blue and silver shades, eryngiums are in a class of their own. They are long-lasting and make good partners for almost any other flowers, lending an air of real distinction to flower arrangements of all kinds and to garden borders too. They even dry well, provided the flowers are gathered when they are in their prime – but be sure to leave some for bees and butterflies, which adore the nectar.

Growing conditions

Eryngiums are mostly fairly drought-tolerant, thanks to their deep tap root – although this can also make them difficult to establish as nursery plants. It can also make them prone to rotting on heavy soils: poor ground generally suits them better. Most garden eryngiums are perennial, though the well-known Eryngium giganteum (see left) is biennial. Many types are inclined to self-sow, especially in gravel, and sometimes they hybridize with interesting results. Choose a spell of damp, showery weather to transplant small seedlings or plant

Eryngium planum – a good choice if you want lots of tiny flowers.

Above: Eryngium alpinum has intricately cut bracts. Left: Eryngium × oliverianum is a more vigorous plant, with spiny, narrow bracts.

new specimens, to give them the best chance of settling in well. When planting bought eryngiums, try to keep as much compost as possible snugly around the root when you remove the plants from their pots.

GOOD ERYNGIUM VARIETIES

Eryngium alpinum (see above) – Beautiful soft, lacy blue bracts surrounding the typical eryngium flowerheads. Tall, blue-tinted stems.

E. bourgatii – Blue flowers and a long season of interesting marbled foliage on a short, tough plant.

E. ebracteatum var. poterioides – A most unusual and rather special eryngium, much more like a sanguisorba, with maroon burrs floating on slender, wiry stems.

E. giganteum (see far left).

E. × oliverianum (see above) – Tall and vigorous, blue-stemmed hybrid with stiff, spiny, narrow bracts framing blue flowers.

E. planum (see left) – Useful sprays of small flowers varying in colour according to cultivar.

E. × tripartitum – Sprays of small flowers, very handy for petite arrangements, fresh or dried.

E. × zabelii – Another vigorous hybrid with a number of cultivars including 'Jos Eijking' and 'Violetta'.

Erysimum 'Bowles's Mauve'
Perennial wallflower

◐❄◇↓↓ pH← —pH↑ ❖ SPRING to SUMMER

H 30–60cm (12–24in) S to 1.2m (4ft)

One of the hardier shrubby wallflowers (but less fragrant than some), E. 'Bowles's Mauve' is reliably perennial in sheltered gardens with good drainage. The flower spikes work well in vases with silver, lime green and violet blue. The plants get leggy in time but are easy to replace from cuttings. Other good varieties: E. 'Apricot Twist', 'Cotswold Gem' and the double golden E. cheiri 'Harpur Crewe'. Some have variegated foliage.

Euonymus fortunei 'Silver Queen'

◐●● ❖ YEAR-ROUND

H and S 2m (6ft)

This invaluable evergreen provides long-lasting, white-variegated foliage all year for arrangements. Happy to cling to a shady wall or tree trunk, it looks good against brickwork and brightens dark corners inside and out. It is slow to establish, but tolerates dry, poor soil, although of course it does better in more favourable conditions. For gold-variegated foliage, the more compact E.f. 'Emerald 'n' Gold' is equally reliable.

Euphorbia amygdaloides var. robbiae Mrs Robb's bonnet

◐●● ✿ ❖ SPRING

H 50cm (20in) S indefinite

This tough perennial is useful for odd corners of the garden and will tolerate dry shade. It will spread freely if you let it, particularly in rich soil. Cut the longer stems to partner other spring flowers in whites and blues. The fresh acid-green flowerheads bring the essence of spring into the house, and they last well. As with all euphorbias, the milky sap is a skin irritant. Trim off faded flowerheads in summer to keep the plant tidier.

Galanthus Snowdrop

◯◐◑♦↓↓ ✿ ❖ EARLY SPRING

H 15cm (6in) S 10cm (4in)

Small bunches of snowdrops indoors are the best reminder that winter is on its way out. Grow the bulbs where they can be left undisturbed, provided it is not too dry or shady. Picked newly open, the flowers last several days. Put them with a few simple, dark green leaves like ivy, hellebores or arums. Early G. 'Atkinsii' is large and vigorous; 'Magnet' (shown above), with its flowers hanging from delicate, arching stems, is the most graceful in a vase.

Galium odoratum
Sweet woodruff

◯◐◑ ❖ LATE SPRING to EARLY SUMMER

H 30cm (12in) S indefinite

Though it is perhaps too invasive for ultra-tidy gardeners, sweet woodruff will quickly cover the ground in difficult, shady spots with a low cushion of green spangled with countless tiny white stars. It appears at just the right time to mask the fading foliage of spring bulbs. Sprigs of it make charming company in a small vase with almost any other spring flowers. Its fragrance when dried led to its use in medieval times as a strewing herb and to scent linen.

Geranium 'Patricia'

◯◐◑♦↓↓ ❖ SPRING to AUTUMN

H and S 60cm (2ft)

Similar to the splendid G. psilostemon, but taking up less space, this reliable perennial is perfect for underplanting with spring bulbs, as its fast-growing mound of attractive leaves in late spring soon hides fading bulb foliage. The flowers give a quick boost to displays and look good with violet-blue and lime green but, like most hardy geraniums, they don't last long once cut.

Geum rivale 'Leonard's Variety'

○ ◐ ● ↕ 🍃 ❖ LATE SPRING

H and S 30cm (12in)

This is one of a group of geums with dainty, nodding blooms in subtle colours in spring – ideal at the front of a cottage-style border. The flowers are short-lived, but the buds and fluffy seedheads are just as pretty. Slightly later-flowering, bolder geums include G. 'Lady Stratheden' (yellow), 'Mrs J. Bradshaw' (red) and 'Prinses Juliana' (orange). Geums like moist, well-drained soil that never dries out. Easy to grow from seed.

Hedera Ivy

○ ◐ ● ❖ YEAR-ROUND

H and S to 3m (10ft) or more

With their evergreen foliage, ivies are very useful all year round for a variety of displays, including Christmas wreaths. *H. helix* 'Glacier' (shown above) is a pretty, easy-to-grow, cream-variegated form. Frilly *H.h.* 'Ivalace' suits dainty posies and slender *H.h.* 'Pedata' trails gracefully. Bolder ivies, like *H. colchica* cultivars, are handy for big arrangements and decorations. Keep ivies trimmed and don't let them root into loose mortar.

Helianthus annuus Sunflower

○ pH↑ ❖ MIDSUMMER to EARLY AUTUMN

H to 4m (13ft) S 45cm (18in)

Most people are familiar with giant sunflowers, but there are many others more suitable for cutting. 'Holiday' is bushy, about 1.2m (4ft) tall, with enough flowers to provide plenty for cutting and still leave some to enhance the garden. 'Velvet Queen' is deep bronze; 'Valentine' (shown above) has pale creamy-yellow flowers; 'Teddy Bear' is dwarf (60cm/2ft), with double, bright yellow pom-poms.

Gypsophila paniculata

○ ◐ ↕ pH← –pH↑ ❖ SUMMER

H and S 60cm (2ft)

Pink and white gypsophilas are classic florist's flowers, with good reason. Their light-as-air texture, with tiny flowers and thread-like stems, contrasts well with more solid flowers, making everything in a bunch look dainty, especially roses and other traditional pastel-coloured flowers. Good varieties include 'Rosenschleier' (pale pink, shown above) and 'Bristol Fairy' (white). Gypsophilas need space and sunshine, so don't allow other plants to swamp them.

Helenium 'Moerheim Beauty'

Sneezeweed

○ ◐ ↕ ❖ LATE SUMMER

H 90cm (3ft) S 60cm (2ft)

The distinctive mop-shaped flowers of heleniums bring splashes of warm colours – yellow, bronze, orange and deep red – to late-summer borders. 'Moerheim Beauty' flowers earlier than others, and will bloom again if cut back after the first flowers fade. Heleniums should be lifted and divided every three years or so. They dislike dry soil and to flower well need plenty of light at the base, so don't let them get crowded out.

Heliotropium arborescens

Cherry pie, Heliotrope

○ ❀ ❖ SUMMER to EARLY AUTUMN

H 45cm (18in) S 30cm (12in)

A warm, sunny corner suits this tender perennial (usually grown as an annual) and is ideal for trapping its fruity scent. Heliotrope is known as cherry pie with good reason – though some plants may be more perfumed than others – and on a sunny windowsill the fragrance will last indoors for a while. It looks good with lime greens and pale yellows. 'Marine' (shown above) is the usual seed strain.

Helleborus × hybridus
Lenten rose

◐ ◉ ♦ ‖ pH← —pH↑ 🌿 ❖ LATE WINTER to SPRING
H and S 45cm (18in)

Grow hellebores (Ashwood Garden hybrids shown above) in a border near the house so you can enjoy their exotic waxy blooms for weeks in the coldest, darkest days of the year. Indoors, the flowers are best displayed by floating them face up in a shallow bowl of water (*see* page 18). The stems tend to droop in a vase, but searing and slitting them at the base can help (*see* page 40).

Hosta 'Sum and Substance'

◐ ◉ ● ♦ ‖ ❖ LATE SPRING to SUMMER
H and S 1m (40in)

Hostas are useless for cutting if their leaves have been spoiled by slugs, as they all too often are. However, 'Sum and Substance' is a huge, robust variety with good slug resistance. Its bold golden-green leaves are a good foil for blues and purples in large arrangements. For something on a much smaller scale, try the petite *H.* 'Ginko Craig', which has pretty variegated leaves and darker flowers than usual. It is easily grown in a pot if slugs are a problem.

Humulus lupulus Hop

○ ◐ ‖ ❖ SPRING, AUTUMN
H and S to 6m (20ft)

Cut the bristly, twining stems of the golden hop, 'Aureus' (shown above), in late spring, while the leaves are young and bright enough to enliven a dark corner. Let them trail prettily from their vase; for an exciting partnership, add violet-blue flowers. Female hops come into their own in autumn with their swags of scented fruits. Hang them in a dry, airy place to use in garlands which, if properly dried, will last all winter.

Hydrangea macrophylla

○ ◐ 🌿 ❖ LATE SUMMER
H 2m (6ft) S 2.5m (8ft)

Hydrangeas are a useful addition to the flower-arranger's repertoire, with large, imposing flowerheads at a time of year when many plants are winding down for winter. Use them fresh, or hang them upside down to air-dry (*see* page 41). They keep their colours well, tending to be blue on acid soil and pink on alkaline. 'Mariesii Perfecta' (shown above) is a pretty lacecap variety; 'Madame Emile Mouillère' is a favourite white mophead.

Hyssopus officinalis Hyssop

○ ‖ ❖ LATE SUMMER to EARLY AUTUMN
H 60cm (2ft) S 90cm (3ft)

Dainty flower spikes in a true, deep blue ensure that this little-known shrubby, fragrant herb is a valuable component of a dry, sunny, late-summer border. Use it in a similar way to lavender in petite arrangements. Cut the plants back quite hard in late spring to keep them neat. Dead-head in summer. Take cuttings to make replacement plants every few years as the old ones turn woody. Hyssop can also be grown from seed.

Iberis Candytuft

○ ‖ pH← —pH↑ ❖ LATE SPRING
H 20cm (8in) S 60cm (24in)

The perennial *I. sempervirens* (shown above) is a trouble-free evergreen, handy for its flat white flowerheads and dark green foliage – good in small vases. Easy to grow, it will spill over a low wall in a sunny, dry spot. The hardy annual *I. umbellata* has similar flowers, also good for cutting. Usually sold as a colourful seed mixture, it is easy and self-sows. Try it at the edge of a border, or in a row in a cutting patch.

Ilex aquifolium 'Handsworth New Silver' Variegated holly

○◑🍂 ❖ YEAR-ROUND

H and S 3m (10ft)

Hollies are such attractive members of the winter garden cast that it is worth growing at least one. It may as well be a dual-purpose variety such as this, with attractive, evergreen, white-edged leaves and berries (if there is a male holly in the vicinity; if there isn't, grow the self-fertile, plain-leaved 'J.C. van Tol'). Hollies can be slow to get going, but should eventually provide a regular supply of winter foliage and Christmas berries for years to come.

Iris foetidissima Stinking iris

◑◐↕ ❖ SUMMER to WINTER

H and S 60cm (2ft)

This tough, easy evergreen perennial is no garden star, but well worth growing in an odd corner for its glowing bunches of orange seeds. A few of these long, fruiting stems displayed in a tall, slender jug or vase make a fine and long-lasting winter arrangement; they also work well in Christmas wreaths and other decorations. Hang the stems upside down for a few days to stiffen and dry out, to help them stay upright.

Iris sibirica Siberian iris

○◑◐💧 ❖ LATE SPRING to EARLY SUMMER

H 60–120cm (2–4ft) S 45cm (18in)

Irises are not long-lived when cut, but *I. sibirica* cultivars, available in a range of beautiful colours and patterns, make good border verticals, and the long-stalked flowers and strap-shaped leaves are a strong element in arrangements. Cut the plants just as the flowers are opening. The blue varieties are the most useful: 'Tropic Night' (deep violet-blue), 'Perry's Blue' (lighter, sky-blue), or 'Flight of Butterflies' (with exquisitely veined falls in violet and white, shown above).

Iris unguicularis Algerian iris

○◊💧↕ ❖ WINTER to EARLY SPRING

H and S 30cm (12in)

Watching the buds of this sun-loving perennial unfurl indoors is a great winter pleasure. The plant takes a while to settle into flowering, but put it in poor, rubbly soil at the base of a sunny wall and forget it except for removing any dead leaves. One mild winter's day it will surprise you with its exotic flowers: light lavender-blue in the species, a deeper violet-blue in the cultivar 'Mary Barnard'.

Jasminum nudiflorum

Winter jasmine

○◑◐●↕ ❖ WINTER

H and S 3m (10ft)

Although winter jasmines easily become straggly, they are forgiven everything in midwinter, when they produce masses of sunny yellow flowers for weeks. Hard frost withers the open flowers, but more buds soon burst to replace them. It's a useful plant for a forgotten corner or a north wall. Train it through an evergreen shrub or *Cotoneaster horizontalis*, or clip it over after flowering – though that will mean shorter stems for cutting.

Knautia macedonica

○↕ pH←—pH↑ ❖ SUMMER

H 90cm (3ft) S 30cm (12in)

This relative of wild scabious has flowers of a most unusual rich burgundy colour that complements many other flowers. The tall, wiry plants take up little lateral space and are almost indestructible once established in a well-drained, sunny place. A flowering season that lasts all summer adds to knautia's credentials as a good cut flower, though it could never be described as showy. Butterflies and other pollinating insects love its nectar.

Kniphofia Red-hot poker
○◐◍⥮ ❖ SUMMER

H 60cm–1.8m (2–6ft) S 45–60cm (18–24in)

Slim, vertical spikes give flower arrangements great presence, and kniphofias are one of the main plants that fill this role from midsummer on. They come in all sizes and colours, from the petite, creamy-white 'Little Maid' (shown above), 60cm (2ft), through yellow and green to the huge red-hot pokers like K. uvaria 'Nobilis', 2m (6ft). K. 'Jenny Bloom' is medium-sized with graceful, slender soft-coral spikes.

Lathyrus odoratus Sweet pea
○◐ ❖ SUMMER to EARLY AUTUMN

H 2m (6ft) S 30cm (12in)

Sweet peas ('Matucana' shown above) are ideal for cutting, not least because the more you pick the more they flower. They can be grown on arches, fences or trellis, as well as cane wigwams or tall, twiggy sticks. Long rows work fine in a vegetable patch or allotment. The strongest plants come from seed sown in autumn, but spring sowing works too. Soak seeds overnight before sowing to speed up germination.

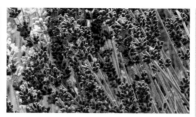

Lavandula angustifolia 'Imperial Gem' Lavender
○◍⥮ ❖ SUMMER

H and S 60cm (2ft)

With violet-blue flowers on a compact, dome-shaped bush, this is the lavender connoisseurs often choose. The foliage is a little more silvery than the better-known 'Hidcote', which is also compact, or 'Munstead', whose flowers are paler – more mauve in colour. Plant several as an edging for a cutting garden or raised bed, and you'll have plenty to cut for use (fresh or dried) and still have some left to attract pollinating bees.

Leucanthemum vulgare Ox-eye daisy
○◐◍◍⥮ ❖ SUMMER to AUTUMN

H 60–90cm (2–3ft) S 30–60cm (12–24in)

A patch of long grass where you have encouraged this easy perennial to grow is a delight of high summer. The long-lasting daisies, with grasses and poppies, are useful for adding a natural look to bunches of country flowers. Cut faded stems to the ground and you should find more flowers later in the year. This also prevents the plant seeding into borders, where it can become too vigorous.

Leucojum aestivum Summer snowflake
○◍ ❖ SPRING

H 75cm (30in) S 30cm (12in)

One of the most spring-like of bulbs, despite its name, this easy plant is perfect for accompanying daffodils and other spring flowers in an arrangement. Its dangling, green-tipped bells are especially good partners for Narcissus 'Jack Snipe'. The flower spikes fade from the top down, but you can simply snip off any withering flowers to keep your arrangement fresh. The similar L. vernum blooms earlier on shorter stems.

Liatris spicata Blazing star, Gayfeather
○◍⥮ ❖ LATE SUMMER

H 60cm (24in) S 30cm (12in)

Liatris owes its unusual shaving-brush shape to the fact that its flower spikes open from the top downwards. Its popularity as a florist's flower is on the increase, and there are now white, violet and pink cultivars as well as the usual mauve of the species. It's an excellent plant for butterflies, so grow enough to pick some spikes and leave others to attract them to the garden.

Lilium regale
○ ‖ ❀ ❖ MIDSUMMER

H 90–120cm (3–4ft) S 30cm (12in)

The great silky, very fragrant trumpets of this elegant lily are among the chief highlights of midsummer. A clump of several bulbs, well grown and securely staked, makes an imposing focal point in the garden or a large pot. For cutting, grow larger clumps so you can remove a few stems without reducing the impact, or grow them in a row in a cutting patch. Look out for the dreaded red lily beetle, which can ruin the display.

Linaria purpurea Purple toadflax
○ ‖ ❖ SUMMER

H 90cm (3ft) S 30cm (12in)

The tall, slender spikes of this cottage-garden perennial come not only in the purple of the species but also in pink (in the cultivar 'Canon Went', shown above) and white ('Springside White'). Easy, drought-tolerant and bee-friendly, they all look pretty growing or cut, either together or with other plants. Look out for self-sown seedlings and move them to where you would like them to grow.

Lonicera periclymenum
Honeysuckle
○ ◑ ❖ LATE SPRING to SUMMER

H 6m (20ft) S 1m (40in)

A few sprigs of honeysuckle indoors are a great, if short-lived, treat and an opportunity to enjoy a classic summer scent at close quarters. 'Belgica' blooms from late spring, and 'Serotina' (shown above) later in the summer. Both have flowers in creamy yellow and deep pink. The newer, long-flowering cultivar 'Graham Thomas' has exceptionally fragrant, creamy-yellow flowers.

Limonium platyphyllum
Sea lavender
○ ◌ ‖ ❖ LATE SUMMER

H and S 50cm (20in)

Its leathery leaves and masses of wind-resistant lavender flowers make this a tough, easy and pretty garden perennial. It has a usefully late season, filling gaps in the garden and providing airy sprays that contrast well with more structural flowers in arrangements. Sea lavender is related to the more familiar annual statice, L. sinuatum, with its larger 'everlasting' flowers, also good for cutting and easy to grow from seed.

Liriope muscari
Blue lilyturf
○ ◑ ◐ ● ◌ ‖ pH← —pH↓ ❖ LATE SUMMER to AUTUMN

H 30cm (12in) S 45cm (18in)

Liriope has neat, slender spikes of tiny, purple, bead-like flowers late in the season, making it a good companion for dwarf sedums and Michaelmas daisies. The jet-black, ribbon-like foliage of Ophiopogon planiscapus 'Nigrescens' also complements it well, especially in the cultivars with variegated leaves, such as L. muscari 'John Burch' or 'Gold-banded'. Liriope makes dense ground cover, and is useful as a neat path-edging in semi-shady areas of the garden.

Lunaria annua Honesty
○ ◑ ◐ ● ◌ ‖ ❖ SPRING to AUTUMN

H and S 90cm (3ft)

Biennial purple honesty is among the first plants to make splashes of bright spring border colour. Variegated forms are valuable for their large, bold leaves splashed with creamy white, especially in shade, but flowering is better in sun. Leave some plants to develop those translucent seed cases that catch the winter sunshine. To use them indoors, peel the outer layers off each seed case to reveal the clean, shiny layer inside. Save the seeds, or let the plants self-sow.

Lupinus Lupin
○ ◑ ↓↓ pH← →pH↓ ❖ EARLY to MIDSUMMER
H 90cm (3ft) **S** 75cm (30in)

Lupins look splendid in vases as well as in the garden. They can be tricky to grow; if you have problems, try growing them from seed and treat them like biennials, planting out in autumn and discarding plants after flowering. Choose a reliable seed strain: the Band of Nobles series (shown above) comes as a mixture or in separate colours. An easier alternative to herbaceous lupins is the shrubby tree lupin *L. arboreus*, with spikes of smaller flowers, usually yellow or blue.

Lychnis chalcedonica
Maltese cross
○ ◑ ↓↓ ❖ SUMMER
H 90cm (3ft) **S** 30cm (12in)

This tall, lanky plant tends to flop in the garden, but its flat-topped posies of summer flowers are useful for cutting because of their colour – a true bright, warm red not found in many perennials. It goes well with dark purple, bronze or silver foliage, and with rich, deep-blue flowers such as salvias or larkspur.

Lythrum virgatum Loosestrife
○ ◑ ◔ ◌ 🍂 ❖ SUMMER to AUTUMN
H 60cm (24in) **S** 45cm (18in)

The wild purple loosestrife (*L. salicaria*) is too much of a thug for most gardens, spreading especially aggressively in damp ground. Its similar but more refined relative *L. virgatum* is a much better bet, offering a long season of slender, more branching flower spikes. Good cultivars include 'Dropmore Purple', 'Rose Queen' and a brighter pink, 'The Rocket'.

Matthiola incana Stock
○ pH↑ ❖ LATE SPRING to MIDSUMMER
H to 45cm (18in) **S** 30cm (12in)

Stocks add a range of beautiful pink, lilac and white shades to a border or a cutting patch, and have a wonderful, clove-like fragrance. The sturdiest plants are generally those that have been grown as biennials, sown in summer and overwintered under glass or in a sheltered place for planting out the following spring. Some varieties, such as the ones called 'ten-week stocks', are suitable for growing as annuals, sown in early spring. Stake taller plants.

Moluccella laevis Bells of Ireland
○ ❖ LATE SUMMER
H 60–75cm (24–30in) **S** 45cm (18in)

Each of the tiny, fragrant white flowers on the spire-like stems of this unusual annual is framed by a large, cup-shaped green calyx, resulting in a strongly structured but subtly coloured plant that makes an elegant partner for other more flamboyant annuals. A traditional favourite with flower arrangers, it can also be dried successfully for use in autumn and winter arrangements.

Monarda
Bee balm, Bergamot, Oswego tea
○ ◑ ◔ ↓↓ 🍂 ❖ SUMMER to EARLY AUTUMN
H and **S** 60cm (2ft)

Their scent, rich colours and unusual hooded flowers have all contributed to the popularity of bergamots. However, many of the familiar old varieties, such as 'Cambridge Scarlet' and 'Croftway Pink', have become very prone to mildew, especially in dry soil. It's best to grow one of the newer, mildew-resistant varieties, such as the white 'Schneewittchen', maroon 'Kardinal' and 'Gardenview Scarlet' (shown above).

Muscari Grape hyacinth
○◑💧‖ ❖ SPRING

H 15cm (6in) S 5cm (2in)

It's worth exploring the many less well-known forms of grape hyacinths. Most are less of a nuisance in the garden than the indestructible *M. armeniacum* (though even that has its uses as a cut flower, if confined to wilder areas). *M.a.* 'Valerie Finnis' (shown above) is a lovely pale blue cultivar which, like white forms such as *M. botryoides* 'Album' and the taller, more vigorous *M. aucheri* 'White Magic', shows up well in dappled shade and in arrangements indoors.

Myrtus communis Myrtle
○❄‖ ❖ YEAR-ROUND

H and S 1.5m (5ft)

The small, glossy, evergreen leaves of myrtle have an elegance and a spicy scent that would make this a perfect foliage plant – if only it were hardier. But sheltered gardens and mild winters suit it well, and if severe cold does brown the leaves, new shoots usually appear from the base by midsummer. The creamy-white flowers appear on mature stems, followed by shapely black berries that usually ripen in time to use with the fragrant leaves at Christmas.

Nepeta 'Six Hills Giant' Catmint
○◑△‖ ❖ LATE SPRING to SUMMER

H and S 90cm (3ft)

The first flowers of this familiar tough, drought-tolerant and ground-covering perennial are already on hand to accompany aquilegias, peonies and irises in late spring. It continues into the rose season, and when the flowers eventually fade the plant can be cut back and will produce new flower spikes in time to partner a whole different range of plants, such as sedums and asters, in late summer. Good value!

Myosotis sylvatica Forget-me-not
○◑ ❖ SPRING to EARLY SUMMER

H and S 15–30cm (6–12in)

The disarming charm of forget-me-nots has made them a garden classic. They are very easy to grow and tend to self-sow, but are easy to pull up if unwanted. It is worth sowing seed of darker varieties, such as the compact 'Victoria Blue', from time to time to help your stock to retain a good colour. They are perfect for small, dainty flower arrangements or as a contrasting 'filler' plant with bolder flowers such as tulips.

Narcissus 'Jack Snipe'
○◑ ❖ EARLY SPRING

H 20cm (8in) S 10cm (4in)

For a combination of pretty looks and sound constitution, this is one of the best daffodils. It is reliable and dainty, even in partial shade, and its small size and earliness mean minimal mess as the leaves fade. Plant it at the back of a border or in grass, in groups big enough to allow you to cut some and leave plenty in the garden. In vases it combines beautifully with euphorbia, blue and white grape hyacinths and chionodoxas.

Nerine bowdenii
○❄‖ ❖ AUTUMN

H 45–60cm (18–24in) S 8cm (3in)

With their large, frilly, sugar-pink flowers bursting open at a time of year when other plants are shutting down for winter, these South African bulbs always seem incredibly exotic. The base of a sheltered, warm wall is the best place to grow them. They also work well in pots as the bulbs like to be crowded. This treatment is especially suitable for more tender nerines, available in white, red and different shades of pink.

Nicandra physalodes
Shoo-fly plant
○ ◌ ‖ ❖ SUMMER to AUTUMN
H to 1.2m (4ft) S to 90cm (3ft)

This fast-growing annual is remarkable for its autumn seedheads, which are preceded by very pretty, but short-lived, lavender-blue flowers. The foliage is coarse and looks its worst after early frosts, but the plant soon becomes a handsome skeleton, with intricately sculpted, purplish-black seedpods hanging in rows from arched stems. The stems dry very well, making unusual Christmas decorations.

Nigella damascena Love-in-a-mist
○ ◌ ‖ ❖ SUMMER
H 45cm (18in) S 30cm (12in)

This delightful cottage-garden annual is a great partner for many other plants. The flowers, usually blue but sometimes white or pink, are not long-lived but they float amid feathery foliage, perfect for indoor arrangements, and soon turn into striking inflated seedpods. 'Miss Jekyll' (above) is a good traditional sky-blue form, and there is a colour mixture called 'Persian Jewels'.

Ophiopogon planiscapus
'Nigrescens' Black lilyturf
○ ◐ ● ‖ ❧ ❖ YEAR-ROUND
H 20cm (8in) S 30cm (12in)

The upper leaf surface of this virtually indestructible little evergreen perennial is almost jet black, so it makes a unique partner for many small flowers. Plants may be slow to spread, but a bonus of mature clumps is bunches of glossy black, berry-like seedpods. Use these, with the long-lasting, narrow leaf-blades, in small late-winter posies to striking effect with snowdrops, early blue scillas and pink *Cyclamen coum*.

Origanum Marjoram
○ ◐ ‖ ❖ SPRING to AUTUMN
H and S 60cm (2ft)

The native wild marjoram, *O. vulgare*, is an aromatic shrubby herb loved by bees and butterflies. Garden cultivars include the variegated 'Country Cream' and the golden 'Aureum'. Both kinds are useful in a cutting patch, for the summer flowers, which make good 'fillers' in arrangements, and for the foliage, at its best in spring and early summer. *O. laevigatum* is larger and showier. Its cultivars 'Herrenhausen' (shown above) and 'Hopleys' are deeper pinkish purple.

Osmanthus
○ ◐ ‖ ❧ ❖ YEAR-ROUND
H and S to 2.5m (8ft)

Osmanthus are easy, slow-growing evergreen shrubs that are good for cutting. *O. delavayi* has small, dark green leaves on arching branches, with scented white flowers in spring. Clip after flowering to keep it compact. *O. × burkwoodii* is similar, while *O. heterophyllus* has larger, holly-like leaves and autumn flowers. Cultivars include 'Goshiki' (shown above), with bronze young shoots and gold-splashed leaves, and cream-variegated 'Variegatus'.

Paeonia lactiflora Peony
○ ◐ ● ‖ ❧ ❖ SPRING to MIDSUMMER
H and S 90cm (3ft)

The season for herbaceous peonies starts when fat red buds emerge from the ground, before the attractive foliage makes its impact. The flowering season is short but glorious. Many gardeners fall in love with this plant, and the blooms do look superb in vases. The fragile-looking double varieties, such as 'Sarah Bernhardt' (shown above) and the white 'Duchesse de Nemours', last fairly well if put into water immediately.

Papaver somniferum
Opium poppy
◯ ❖ SUMMER to AUTUMN
H 90cm (3ft) S 45cm (18in)

The fleeting, fragile beauty of any poppy flowers makes them worth bringing indoors and conditioning, if only for a couple of days (*see* page 40). Opium poppies have the bonus of shapely seedheads, which last well if picked and dried when new. The flowers also come in a wonderful range of colours and forms. Save seed from the best; it won't produce identical plants, but it's exciting to find a really good form.

Pennisetum villosum Feathertop
◯ ‡‡ ❖ SUMMER to AUTUMN
H 60cm (24in) S 30cm (12in)

With various 'bottlebrush' flowerheads, pennisetums include some of the prettiest small grasses. Like most fluffier and more dramatic species, *P. villosum* is slightly tender. Consequently, it is often grown from seed like an annual. Pot up a few good plants in autumn, and keep them under cover over winter. The long-haired flowerheads last well and are good for cutting.

Penstemon
◯ ◑ ‡‡ ❖ LATE SUMMER to AUTUMN
H and S 45–90cm (18in–3ft)

Penstemons are long-lived stalwarts of late summer and autumn, flowering for months if dead-headed, and they are easy to propagate from cuttings. There are lots of cultivars in a wide colour range. A tough one is 'Andenken an Friedrich Hahn' (also known as 'Garnet', shown above), in ruby-crimson; 'Evelyn' is shorter and mid-pink; 'Stapleford Gem' is lilac; 'Raven' and 'Blackbird' are both moody purple.

Perovskia atriplicifolia
Russian sage
◯ ◊ ‡‡ ❖ LATE SUMMER to AUTUMN
H 1.2m (4ft) S 60cm (2ft)

This is an indispensable plant for sunny, dry gardens, with its aromatic silver foliage and haze of lavender-blue flowers late in the season. The flower spikes are versatile for cutting: use them whole in big arrangements or cut sideshoots for posies. The plant keeps its interest after flowering, fading to a ghostly skeleton that lasts into winter. It needs space around it and dislikes being crowded in a border; gravel suits it well.

Persicaria amplexicaulis
'Firetail' Bistort
◯ ◑ ◦ ❖ SUMMER to AUTUMN
H and S 90cm (3ft)

Long-lasting, vivid crimson flower spikes are the reason for growing this reliable, rather beefy perennial. It is useful for its long season of colour, but be prepared to keep it in check. It is best in a large border, with other vigorous perennials and shrubs that can hold their own in a crowd. Other similar cultivars include *P.a.* 'Alba' (white), 'Blackfield' (dark red) and 'Taurus' (deep pinkish red).

Phalaris arundinacea var. picta
Gardener's garters, Ribbon grass
◯ ◑ ◦ ❖ LATE SPRING to SUMMER
H 90cm (3ft) S indefinite

This attractive cottage-garden grass is easy to grow, needing only to be kept from swamping its neighbours. The cultivar 'Feesey' is less vigorous. The fine white variegation on the upright, ribbon-like leaves shows up well in dappled shade, complementing whites, and will add a light, vertical touch to a bunch of flowers. This grass also works with blues, and in subtle green schemes with *Alchemilla mollis* and large hostas.

Philadelphus 'Silberregen'
○ ◐ ⊥⊥ ❖ SUMMER

H and S 1.5m (5ft)

The heady fragrance of philadelphus is essential to the magic of a summer garden. Some of the common varieties grow very large and have leaves that are dull – and look coarse in a vase. But P. 'Silberregen' (also sold as 'Silver Showers') is a more delicate shrub, with dainty, scented flowers and small leaves. P. coronarius 'Variegatus' extends the season of interest with white-variegated leaves; P.c. 'Aureus' has golden leaves.

Phlox paniculata Perennial phlox
○ ◐ ♦ ⊥⊥ ⚘ ❖ MIDSUMMER to MID-AUTUMN

H and S 1.2m (4ft)

Perennial phlox keep a garden looking luxuriant into late summer. The species P. paniculata has lilac flowers and there are myriad cultivars in shades of pink, mauve and white, some very fragrant. Well-known forms include: 'Norah Leigh' (shown above) and 'Harlequin' (red-purple), both with variegated leaves, and 'Mount Fuji' (white).

Pittosporum tenuifolium
○ ◐ ❄ ⊥⊥ ❖ YEAR-ROUND

H 1–6m (3–20ft) S 0.6–3m (2–10ft)

Slender dark stems, tiny fragrant flowers and shiny, fluttering evergreen leaves make this one of the most pleasing foliage shrubs. There are various leaf colours, from dark purple ('Purpureum' and the compact 'Tom Thumb') to near yellow ('Warnham Gold'), with many variegated cultivars such as delicate 'Irene Paterson' (shown above) and P. 'Garnettii'. Pittosporums generally are slightly tender, but are worth trying in all but the coldest gardens.

Phlomis russeliana
○ ◐ ⊥⊥ ❖ SUMMER to WINTER

H 1m (40in) S 90cm (3ft)

The sculptured, tiered seedheads of this robust, ground-covering perennial are among the most durable of all, lasting up to a year in the garden. The tall, erect spires look striking covered in frost or snow. Cut some to dry for their impact in autumn arrangements and Christmas decorations. The yellow summer flowers are unusual but hardly refined. Pink-flowered P. italica and P. tuberosa might be easier to use for cutting but are less resistant to cold, wet winters.

Physalis alkekengi Chinese lantern
○ ◐ ⊥⊥ ❖ AUTUMN

H 60cm (2ft) S indefinite

Physalis is very easy but needs careful placing: grow it in a wild area, at the back of a big border or among shrubs. It is quite invasive, and contributes little until autumn. But then, its abundant, jolly orange-red lanterns not only make the garden sing, they cheer up the house all winter. Use stems fresh in autumn, then dry them flat to preserve the gently arching stems and stand a bunch in a large jug. They are great for Christmas decorations (see page 63).

Polemonium 'Lambrook Mauve' Jacob's ladder
○ ◐ ♦ ⊥⊥ ⚘ ❖ EARLY SUMMER

H and S 45cm (18in)

The typical Jacob's ladder of cottage gardens is blue or sometimes white, but this attractive, healthy cultivar with shorter stems has delicate mauve flowers for a longer season. (As a sterile hybrid, unlike the species, it isn't in a hurry to get flowering over with so that it can set seed.) It will grow in pretty well any soil, and its upright habit makes it suitable for the front of a border.

Polygonatum × *hybridum*
Solomon's seal

◑◉♦‡‡ ❖ LATE SPRING to EARLY SUMMER

H 90cm (3ft) S 60cm (2ft)

This favourite woodland plant has elegant, arching stems hung with green and white flowers – as lovely in dappled shade in the garden as in a vase. Cultivars with leaf variations include 'Betberg', whose foliage is light chocolate-brown if grown in good light, and the variegated 'Striatum'. Sawfly caterpillars can be a persistent problem: if you spot leaf damage, search for the culprits and pick them off.

Potentilla Cinquefoil

○◑‡‡ ❖ SUMMER

H and S 30cm (12in)

Herbaceous potentillas have exquisite flowers in a variety of colours, mostly pink, red, yellow and orange. They look good in a vase, even though they are short-lived. The leaves are attractive too, especially those with a silvery sheen. *P. nepalensis* 'Miss Willmott' (shown above) has flowers of an unusual coral colour with a dark eye. *P.* 'Gibson's Scarlet' has jewel-like scarlet flowers and rich-green leaves.

Primula vulgaris Primrose

○◑◑♦‡‡ ❖ SPRING

H 15cm (6in) S 30cm (12in)

There's nothing quite like a freshly picked bunch of primroses to capture the feeling of spring. They are easy to grow and last surprisingly well in water. Primroses can lend a woodland feel to a corner of the garden, where they will often happily self-sow, but you can also dig up a plant or two after flowering and split them into the component rosettes of leaves and roots. Replant, water well, and next year you'll have more.

Pulmonaria Lungwort

◑◑◉♦‡‡ ❖ SPRING

H and S 30cm (12in)

Pulmonarias are one of the first herbaceous perennials to bring colour to spring borders, with flowers in blue, pink, red and in-between shades. The best also make good ground-covering foliage plants later in the year. 'Diana Clare' (shown above) is one such – vigorous, with large, silvered leaves that look good for months and are useful for cutting, and purple flowers. Other good pulmonarias include 'Lewis Palmer' (deep-blue flowers, spotty leaves) and 'Blue Ensign' (plain-leaved).

Pulsatilla vulgaris Pasque flower

○◇‡‡ ❖ SPRING to EARLY SUMMER

H and S 20–30cm (8–12in)

The pasque flower's jewel-like colours – velvety purple, burgundy, mauve or white, with a central boss of vivid golden stamens – are easy to appreciate in uncrowded spring borders. They are better still in a vase. The plant's season of interest is extended by the attractively divided leaves and charming fluffy seedheads on long stems. Save the ripe seed before discarding the flowerheads: when it's fresh, it germinates quite easily. Pasque flower is good for dry gardens.

Rhamnus alaternus 'Argenteovariegata'

○‡‡ ❖ YEAR-ROUND

H and S 2m (6ft)

This pretty, evergreen foliage shrub has neat, dainty little ivory-edged leaves that make it one of the best variegated plants for a sunny garden, and for cutting for arrangements large or small. In a vase it works especially well with blues, purples and deep reds. In winter, look out for the tiny red berries that make the shrub an ideal choice for small-scale Christmas decorations.

Rosa 'Golden Celebration'

○◐ ❖ SUMMER to AUTUMN

H and S 1.2m (4ft)

'Golden Celebration' is a fine, fragrant English rose for cutting, tolerating partial shade and being resistant to disease. It produces its exceptionally large, rich golden-yellow flowers over a long season. It is ideal for when you want a few roses for impact in a mixed arrangement and is lovely with dark blues, and with silver, purple or bronze foliage. Keep dead-heading.

Rosmarinus officinalis Rosemary

○◐⏚ ❖ YEAR-ROUND

H and S 60–180cm (2–6ft)

Providing year-round sprigs of upright, aromatic foliage for cooking as well as arranging, rosemary deserves a place in any dry, sunny spot. A sheltered spot is best for choice cultivars with deep-blue flowers; those of the ordinary, hardier varieties are pale greyish blue. A useful form for tight spaces is 'Miss Jessopp's Upright'. Trim bushes in late spring, after flowering; they dislike hard pruning.

Rosa (Rose)

Roses as cut flowers

Roses are not the easiest flowers to grow, or the longest-lasting when cut, but to be able to enjoy the beauty and fragrance of home-grown roses in the house is a special privilege that can't be ignored. Remember that you are not aiming for the 'dozen perfect blooms' of the florist's shop. Home-grown roses offer variety and fragrance that commercial ones can't, so make the most of them by cutting them in small quantities for mixed arrangements, or display them singly, or in threes or fives, in small vases. Try to arrange them so that their heavy heads are supported by other flowers, or better still cut the stems short and display them in a shallow bowl. Roses often droop if cut with long stems, but can sometimes be revived by soaking them up to their necks overnight.

Single roses

Single roses are often overlooked when it comes to cutting. It's true that they're short-lived, and usually short-stemmed too, but they have a lovely uncomplicated charm that no double rose can match. Cut them just as they are opening, and enjoy their beauty indoors for a few days by arranging a handful of the flowers in a shallow container, supported by a bed of foliage sprigs or *Alchemilla mollis*. This works well with the gorgeous red *Rosa* 'Geranium' (try it with silver foliage from *Elaeagnus* 'Quicksilver' and blue hardy geraniums), the early yellow *R. xanthina* 'Canary Bird', or even simple wild dog roses. The method is also a good way to display the many beautiful double roses that don't have strong stems.

A bowl of roses: the essence of summer.

GOOD ROSE VARIETIES

Rosa 'Gertrude Jekyll' – Reliable, tall, repeat-flowering English rose with highly fragrant, rich-pink flowers that last well in water.

R. 'Golden Celebration' (*see* far left).

R. 'Graham Thomas' – Robust, well-scented yellow English rose that can be grown either as a bush or as a compact climber.

R. 'Just Joey' – Fragrant, coppery-orange Hybrid Tea rose on a fairly compact bush. Produces flowers continuously for a long season.

R. 'Madame Alfred Carrière' – Robust, vigorous Climbing rose with scented, blush-white flowers for a long season. Tolerates light shade.

R. 'New Dawn' – Repeat-flowering Climbing rose with glossy leaves and pale pink, fragrant blooms.

R. 'Royal William' – Velvety-red, robust Hybrid Tea rose with dark green leaves and some scent.

R. 'The Fairy' – Healthy, dwarf Shrub rose that flowers abundantly all summer, giving a reliable supply of small, double pink roses ideal for posies and small arrangements.

R. 'William Shakespeare 2000' – Full-flowered, strongly fragrant, rich magenta-crimson blooms on a compact, upright bush.

Rudbeckia Coneflower
○◑♦ ❖LATE SUMMER
H 0.6–2m (2–6ft) S 60–90cm (2–3ft)

There are both perennial and annual forms of these daisies, nearly all giving late-season borders (and vases) a boost of colour. Perennial types are yellow, ranging in height from 2m (6ft) as in the case of *R. laciniata* 'Herbstsonne' (shown above), with slightly drooping petals and a green cone, to 75cm (30in) in *R. fulgida* var. *sullivantii* 'Goldsturm' (with a black cone). *R. occidentalis* 'Green Wizard' has no petals, just a big, brown central boss with a ruff of green bracts.

Salix Willow
○◑♦ ❖WINTER to SPRING
H and S according to species

The ornamental potential of willows includes the velvety spring leaf-buds, familiar as 'pussy willow' in the wild goat willow (*S. caprea*) and the florist's *S. gracilistyla* 'Melanostachys'. This and other more compact trees, including *S. daphnoides* (shown above), also have colourful bark. Some willows, like the bushy shrub *S. lanata,* have lovely silver foliage. *S. babylonica* var. *pekinensis* 'Tortuosa' is a tall tree whose bare, curly stems make it a sculptural winter feature.

Salvia viridis Annual clary
○◑ ❖SUMMER to AUTUMN
H 40–45cm (16–18in) S 30cm (12in)

The flowers of this familiar, easy, hardy annual are unimpressive, but the leaf-like bracts in pink, violet-blue or white, with contrasting green veins, make the stems a colourful companion for other flowers, both in borders and in vases. It also dries well. Seeds are available in the individual colours or as a mixture. The blue shades work especially well with strong reds and oranges, and with euphorbias, *Alchemilla mollis* and white daisies.

Sanguisorba Burnet
○◑♦ ❖SUMMER to AUTUMN
H 0.3–2m (1–6ft) S 20–50cm (8–20in)

Sanguisorbas are perennials with colourful burrs on wiry stems. Varieties vary widely in height, colour, burr shape and soil requirements. Another variable is the seedheads: choose a form where they are long-lasting and attractive, such as the white-flowered 'Burr Blanc' (1.2m/4ft). 'Tanna' (shown above), with dark red burrs, is good at the front of a border and for small arrangements (30cm/12in). *S. tenuifolia* 'Pink Elephant' (2m/6ft) is large with pink flowers.

Santolina chamaecyparissus
Cotton lavender
○⌇ ❖SUMMER to AUTUMN
H and S 75cm (30in)

This compact, aromatic shrub offers good value for space in a sunny area. Easy to grow, it provides sprigs of feathery silver foliage all year and, in summer, small, bright yellow button flowers on stiff stems. These actually look better in a mixed posy than on the bush, and they dry well. 'Lemon Queen' has pale yellow flowers. For bright green leaves, try *S. rosmarinifolia* and its paler-flowered cultivar 'Primrose Gem'.

Sarcococca confusa Christmas box
◑●⌇🍃 ❖WINTER to EARLY SPRING
H and S 1.2m (4ft)

Few plants can put a difficult area of dense shade to such good use as this compact shrub, which has powerfully fragrant white flowers very early in the year. It always looks neat, with its shiny, evergreen foliage covering the ground, suppressing weeds. Cut sprigs are an ideal partner for snowdrops, scillas and *Cyclamen coum*. By midsummer, the flowers have become dark red berries that ripen to shiny black.

Scabiosa caucasica 'Clive Greaves'

○◇↕ pH← —pH↑ ❖ SUMMER to AUTUMN

H and S 45cm (18in)

This scabious is a lovely perennial border plant and offers a long season of lavender-blue flowers on wiry stems. It has traditionally been a favourite with flower arrangers – and, like all scabious, with the butterflies and bees, which are attracted by its nectar. It lasts well in water if it is cut just as the buds are beginning to burst. *S. caucasica* 'Miss Willmott' has white flowers.

Scilla mischtschenkoana

○◑ ❖ EARLY SPRING

H and S 15cm (6in)

Its early flowering season – before other scillas and chionodoxas – is what makes this hardy little bulb worth a place in any garden. It can be tucked away at the back of a border or under shrubs, and will flower reliably for years, even in partial shade, where its unassuming, pale ice-blue flowers show up best. Good partners for it, in the garden and in little posies indoors, are *Cyclamen coum*, snowdrops and pulmonarias.

Sedum Herbstfreude Group 'Herbstfreude'

○◇↕ ❖ LATE SUMMER to LATE WINTER

H and S 60cm (2ft)

One of the best late-summer border perennials (also known as 'Autumn Joy'), this reliable sedum, or 'ice plant', makes an attractive silvery-green background plant all summer before its coral flowerheads open and then gradually fade into russet seedheads that last all winter. Flowers and seedheads are long-lasting when cut. Plant several along the front of a dry, sunny border.

Skimmia

◑●◌🍃 ❖ WINTER to SPRING

H and S 1.5m (5ft)

Skimmias are evergreen and as attractive in bud as in flower, though male clones like *S. japonica* 'Rubella' (shown above) have no berries. This compact cultivar has clusters of long-lasting, deep-red flower buds, useful for cutting in winter. *S. × confusa* 'Kew Green' (also male) has more subtle green buds and white flowers. Both are very fragrant. Female varieties with red berries include *S. japonica* 'Nymans' and the dwarf 'Red Riding Hood'. There are also white-berried cultivars.

Solidago rugosa 'Fireworks'

○◑♦↕ ❖ LATE SUMMER to AUTUMN

H 1.2m (4ft) S 60cm (2ft)

The ordinary golden rod (*S. rugosa*) has a short flowering season, scarcely justifying its nuisance value as it spreads and seeds where you don't want it, but some forms are useful for cutting. *S. rugosa* 'Fireworks' has the typical yellow flowers but in long, slender arching spikes on an airy 1.2m (4ft) plant. A more dwarf variety, flowering slightly earlier, is *S.* 'Goldenmosa'. 'Goldkind' is smaller still, at 60cm (2ft).

Spiraea thunbergii

○◑↕ ❖ SPRING

H and S 1.8m (6ft)

With its slim, arching sprays of countless tiny white flowers, this early-blooming spiraea is sure to create a most graceful, spring-like effect in an arrangement with bulbs and pulmonarias or other early flowers. Although quite an ordinary shrub, it is less widely available than other spiraeas that flower a little later, but it's worth tracking down. Prune it after flowering to encourage an upright shape, which will show next year's flowers to best effect.

Stachys officinalis 'Hummelo'
○ ‖ ❖ SUMMER
H 60cm (24in) S 30cm (12in)

The native betony, *S. officinalis*, is a grassland wildflower with reddish-purple spikes of lipped flowers a little like orchids. This lilac-purple cultivar has larger flowers but is easy to grow and reliable. 'Rosea Superba' is a purer pink, and 'Alba' and 'Wisley White' are useful whites. With their upright, unbranched flower spikes and tidy, healthy-looking green foliage, they lend themselves to cutting and are mostly trouble-free.

Tanacetum parthenium
'Aureum' Golden feverfew
○ ◐ ‖ ❖ SPRING to SUMMER
H and S 30cm (12in)

This is a useful perennial to have around. It is short-lived, but keeps going by self-sowing on light soil without being a nuisance, providing patches of bright golden foliage from early spring. It works well near blue aquilegias and irises, complementing their colours and gently taking over as they fade. White, daisy-like feverfew flowers arrive around midsummer – ideal 'filler' material for small to medium-sized arrangements.

Tellima grandiflora
○ ◐ ◌ ❖ SPRING to MIDSUMMER
H 80cm (32in) S 30cm (12in)

Vertical spikes with tough, wiry stems are so useful for giving support and shape in arrangements that it's a pity not to make use of this shade-loving, unfussy ground-cover plant with its long-lasting crop of just such flowers. The individual flowers along each spike are highly delicate; the lacy ruff framing each tiny flower starts out greenish ivory but often turns deep pink later, adding a warm hue that picks up related flower colours in an arrangement.

Tricyrtis formosana Toad lily
◐ ● ◌ ‖ pH← –pH↓ ❖ LATE SUMMER to AUTUMN
H 80cm (32in) S 60cm (24in)

With their intricately structured flowers in subtle colours and patterns, tricyrtis are a bit special and positively demand to be viewed at close quarters. One stem makes a good single specimen in a bud vase, especially a spotted form such as *T. formosana*. They are quite tricky to grow, needing sheltered woodland conditions with leafy, neutral to acid soil and a mild climate – but worth a go!

Triteleia laxa 'Koningin Fabiola'
○ ‖ ❖ SUMMER
H 30cm (12in) S 8cm (3in)

This midsummer-flowering bulb seems tailor-made for cutting, each leafless, rigid stem supporting a cluster of strikingly bright flowers like miniature blue lilies. Buy plenty of bulbs, if you can find them – they are inexpensive, and take up little space – to plant in autumn. An easy plant for a sunny cutting patch, it also works well in containers of gritty, free-draining compost. Just as charming, *T. ixioides* 'Starlight' produces subtly striped cream flowers slightly earlier.

Tropaeolum majus Nasturtium
○ ◐ ❖ SUMMER to AUTUMN
H and S 0.3–1.5m (1–5ft)

Nasturtiums can be used to take over from early perennials, quickly filling their place with a scrambling mass of orange, yellow and red to last until autumn frosts. Bright flowers and edible leaves make all varieties good for cutting. The flowers don't last long but the plants are prolific. They look good with the deep-blue spikes of salvias or hyssop. Seeds self-sow and remain viable in the soil over winter, making strong plants.

Tulipa 'Ballerina'
○ ‖ ❖ LATE SPRING
H 50cm (20in) S 15cm (6in)

This elegant, robust, Lily-flowered tulip makes a real impact in a border or cutting patch, or even in a large pot. Orange is uncommon in the spring garden, so it's exciting to put together a few of these lovely tulips in a vibrant mixture with dark blue and lime green. They also look good with purple foliage: grow 'Ballerina' with bronze fennel or an ornamental elder such as *Sambucus nigra* 'Gerda' ('Black Beauty').

Verbena bonariensis
○ ‖ ❖ LATE SUMMER to AUTUMN
H 1.5m (5ft) S 45cm (18in)

Who would be without this invaluable late-season perennial, so attractive to butterflies and so flattering to borders and arrangements? It is instrumental in prolonging summer colour – sometimes until late autumn – and its tall, slender stems and small, compact flowerheads mean it seldom gets in the way of other plants. It's a keen self-sower, particularly in sheltered gardens with light soil (it dislikes wet, cold soil in winter).

Tulipa (Tulip)

Left: Sumptuous *Tulipa* 'Black Hero'. Right: Cool, sophisticated *Tulipa* 'Spring Green'.

Stars of spring
Tulips are right up there with the very best plants to grow for cutting. The flowers are dramatic and the stems sturdy, and the range of colours, sizes and shapes is huge. You can have tulips in flower from late winter almost until summer. They are straightforward to grow, and usually flower reliably, in their first year at least. Tulips do well in a container, where they can be used to create a striking focal point in the garden, and they are perfectly happy growing in rows for cutting, in an allotment, vegetable patch or cutting garden. Plenty of light and reliably well-drained soil are their only requirement. For details of how to condition tulips after cutting, *see* page 40.

Species tulips
Amid the large, highly bred cultivated tulips that tend to steal the show, don't overlook the more compact, dainty wild species that are available. They include the very earliest to flower, such as dwarf white *Tulipa polychroma* and the taller, tough, cream *T. turkestanica*, which goes on to produce attractive seedheads. The latest tulip to flower is *T. sprengeri*, with elegant pointed petals in bright scarlet. Many species, such as early red *T. praestans* and pink or purple *T. humilis*, will flower reliably for years given the free-draining conditions that are essential to their success. As with all bulbs, make sure your tulips have been sustainably sourced and not taken from wild places.

GOOD TULIP VARIETIES

Tulipa 'Abu Hassan' – Rich mahogany-red flowers with a golden edge to the petals.

T. 'Apeldoorn' – Large, strong, early, cherry-red. Lasts well from year to year.

T. 'Ballade' – Tall, strikingly elegant Lily-flowered tulip with deep purplish-pink petals margined in white.

T. 'Ballerina' (*see* far left).

T. 'Black Hero' (*see* above) – Double and tall, with large, very dark purplish-black flowers. Robust, long-lasting.

T. 'Bleu Aimable' – Not blue but the closest a tulip gets: lilac-mauve, with broad flowers on very tall stems. 'Blue Parrot' is similar but frilly.

T. 'China Pink' – Reliable, long-lived, satiny-pink, Lily-flowered variety.

T. 'Prinses Irene' – Early, compact and neat, with unusual colouring of orange suffused with purple. Looks very striking against a backdrop of purple foliage.

T. 'Purissima' – Very large, early white flowers, good with spring yellows, blues and whites.

T. 'Spring Green' (*see* above) – Subtle green-and-ivory tulip, the very essence of spring in a border. Harmonizes well with other plants.

T. 'West Point' – Sturdy, bright yellow, Lily-flowered tulip with long, elegant petals that open wide in sunshine.

Veronica spicata Spiked speedwell
○ ⬇⬇ ❖ EARLY SUMMER
H 30–60cm (12–24in) S 30cm (12in)

Perennials with vertical flower spikes play a vital role in arrangements, and the veronicas include a wide variety of such plants. The upright *V. spicata* is blue, but it has cultivars in other colours, such as the striking, deep-pink 'Rotfuchs' (shown above), 'Romiley Purple' and 'Snow White'. Some other forms are very dwarf. Another lovely, earlier-flowering species with erect spikes is the dainty *V. gentianoides*, available in blue or white.

Viburnum tinus Laurustinus
○ ◑ ● ❖ EARLY WINTER to SPRING
H and S 2.5m (8ft)

Although it is a reliable workhorse rather than a plant to arouse excitement, a laurustinus covered in buds is a pretty and promising sight in late winter. Its evergreen foliage is serviceable but dull, yet in a shady corner or at the back of a large border it can be useful for screening. 'Eve Price' and 'Gwenllian' (shown above) have deep-pink buds and pink-tinged flowers; 'French White' shows up well in shade. Trim after flowering.

Vinca difformis Periwinkle
○ ◑ ● ❖ LATE AUTUMN to SPRING
H 30cm (12in) S indefinite

Early-flowering *V. difformis* has a usefully long season, usually starting in late autumn. The milky-white flowers may not last long indoors, but in mild spells there will be more to cut. Cultivars of lesser periwinkle, *V. minor*, are equally lovely, and useful as ground cover, with their main flowering season in spring: *V.m.* 'La Grave' is blue; in shade try the white *V.m.* f. *alba* 'Gertrude Jekyll'. Don't allow periwinkles to take over.

Viola cornuta Horned violet
○ ◑ ● pH← —pH↑ ✤ SUMMER
H 15cm (6in) S 30cm (12in)

Violas come in a fascinating array of patterns and colours so, although they don't last long in water, putting a few in a tiny vase that can be viewed close up is a good way to see their 'faces' and to enjoy the fragrance of scented varieties. In the garden, blue or white *V. cornuta* and its cultivars are useful for visually knitting a border together, scrambling among other plants and popping up in gaps. Violas freely cross-pollinate, often with interesting results.

Zantedeschia aethiopica Arum lily
○ ◑ ❄ ● ❖ LATE SPRING to EARLY SUMMER
H and S 90cm (3ft)

A few pure white arum lilies in a vase make a real statement. Sophisticated and formal, they can look magical when carefully positioned and well lit. They are not always easy to grow, needing moist, fertile soil and disliking intense cold in winter. They can be grown in shallow water or in a big container. The cultivar 'Crowborough' (shown above) is hardier and more resilient in dry soil than some.

Zinnia
○ ❀ ❖ SUMMER to AUTUMN
H and S 30–90cm (1–3ft)

Growing zinnias is a gamble, but they are the perfect plants for an Indian summer – their intense colours looking magnificent in low, late-summer sunshine – so take a chance and hope conditions will be right. Flower arrangers favour the subtle chartreuse-green 'Envy' (shown above). Zinnias need warm weather, hating cold and wet. Sow seed in late spring, when nights are warmer, and feed and water consistently to make bushy plants by midsummer.

Index

Page numbers in *italics* refer to plants in the Recommended plants for cutting directory.

Acknowledgements

BBC Books and OutHouse would like to thank the following for their assistance in preparing this book: Andrew McIndoe for advice and guidance; Robin Whitecross for picture research; Lesley Riley for proofreading; Marie Lorimer for the index.

Picture credits

Key t = top, b = bottom, l = left, r = right, c = centre

PHOTOGRAPHS

All photographs by Jonathan Buckley unless listed below.

David Austin 86tl

GAP Photos Maxine Adcock 38(3), 59(1); Thomas Alamy 38(2), 39(4), 75br; Matt Anker 39(3), 58b, 77bc; Lee Avison 51t(1), 88bc; Pernilla Bergdahl 49b, 53r, 65br, 73bc, 87bc; Rebecca Bernstein 13; Dave Bevan 39(5), 70tc, 71tc, 83br, 89tc; Elke Borkowski 11l, 39(1), 49tr, 56t & b, 70tl, 78tc, 80br; Adrian Bloom 70bc; Richard Bloom 22h, 49tl, 58tl, 59(3), 69tr, 77bl, 85bc; Mark Bolton 39(2), 51bl(1) & (2); Christa Brand 11cl, 15tl, 47b; Nicola Browne 20br, 73tl; Jonathan Buckley 75tr, 87tc, 91br; Chris Burrows 47t, 67tr; Leigh Clapp 63(1), 71br; Marg Cousens 88bl; Julie Dansereau 21g, 71tl; Claire Davies 84br; Frederic Didillon 21f, 69bc, 89br; David Dixon 48b, 63(3); Geoff du Feu 23a; Heather Edwards 54br, 61tl; Ron Evans 15b, 23h, 74bl; FhF Greenmedia 80bc; Victoria Firmston 38(1), 70tr; Tim Gainey 73br; GAP Photos 50b, 63br; Suzie Gibbons 24; John Glover 21b, 22e, 22g, 23b, 32, 61cl, 62bc; Manuela Goehner 19tl & tc; Lucy Griffiths 54b; Anne Green-Armytage 15tr; Charles Hawes 77tl; Martin Hughes-Jones 54tr, 59(2), 65tr, 68bc, 74br, 76tr, 82bc, 83tc, 84tl, 91tl; Jerry Harpur 29, 72tl; Marcus Harpur 20bl, 72tr, 78tl, 87tl; Neil Holmes 17br, 21h, 23c, 61tr, 75tl, 82tr, 91bl; Michael Howes 67bc;

Jason Ingram 71tr; Lynn Keddie 63(2), 72br; Fiona Lea 19b; Jenny Lilly 22a, 23e; Fiona McLeod 60b, 85br; Zara Napier 61br; Clive Nichols 22d; Abigail Rex 84bl; Howard Rice 51t(2), 88br; Sabina Ruber 63bl; S & O 71bl, 71bc, 73tr, 78tr; JS Sira 11r, 62bl, 75tc, 76br, 79bl, 80tl, 88tl, 89tr; Jan Smith 68tr, 85bl; Martin Staffler 30; Friedrich Strauss 48t, 52t, 55b, 60t, 64, 80tr; Graham Strong 5l, 53l; Maddie Thornhill 39(6); Tommy Tonsberg 50tl; Visions 20t, 82tr; Juliette Wade 53c, 74tr, 81bc; Jo Whitworth 12, 17tr, 21e, 31r, 50tr, 87bl; Dave Zubraski 72bc, 79br, 89tl

Garden Collection Andrew Lawson 8; John Glover 17tl, 62br; Marie O'Hara 86r; Neil Sutherland 2/3

Andrew McIndoe 62t

Marianne Majerus Garden Images 10, 52b

Robin Whitecross 18(1), 66tl, 78bc, 83tl, 91tc

ILLUSTRATIONS

Julia Cady 25, 26

Lizzie Harper 36tl & tr, 44, 45a, c, d, e, f & g

Sue Hillier 45b

Thanks are also due to the following designers and owners, whose gardens appear in the book: Jo de Nobriga 24; Timothy Easton 29; Wendy & Leslie Howell 31tl; Christopher Lloyd, Great Dixter, East Sussex 11c, 14b; Ulf Nordfell 13; Piet Oudolf 17tr; Sarah Raven, Perch Hill, East Sussex 9, 14t, 16t, 17tc & bl, 18bl & br, 19tr, 28, 38t, 40, 46, 55(1); Scott Arboretum, Swathmore College, PA, USA 59(3); Matthew Spriggs 63(1); Sarah Taylor 31r; RHS Wisley 71tl

While every effort has been made to trace and acknowledge all copyright holders, the publisher would like to apologize should there be any errors or omissions.